Keto Diet for Beginners 2023

The Complete Guide to Ketogenic Diet for Beginners with 21-Day Meal Plan and Over 100 Simple Recipes

PATRICIA BOHN

Copyright © 2023 Patricia Bohn
All rights reserved.

No part of this publication may be reproduced, distributed, or transmitted in any form or by any means, including photocopying, recording, or other electronic or mechanical methods, except as permitted by U.S. copyright law.

Legal Notice:

This book is copyright protected. This book is only for personal use. You cannot amend, distribute, sell, use, quote or paraphrase any part, or the content within this book, without the consent of the author or publisher.

Disclaimer Notice:

Please note the information contained within this document is for educational and entertainment purposes only. All effort has been executed to present accurate, up to date, and reliable, complete information. No warranties of any kind are declared or implied. Readers acknowledge that the author is not engaging in the rendering of legal, financial, medical or professional advice. The content within this book has been derived from various sources. Please consult a licensed professional before attempting any techniques outlined in this book.

Although the author and publisher have made every effort to ensure that the information in this book was correct at press time, the author and publisher do not assume and hereby disclaim any liability to any party for any loss, damage, or disruption caused by errors or omissions, whether such errors or omissions result from negligence, accident, or any other cause.

CONTENTS

INTRODUCTION 1
HOW TO GET STARTED WITH THE KETOGENIC DIET? 2
THE SCIENCE BEHIND KETO 5
BEST FOODS TO FIT INTO THE KETO DIET 10
FOOD TO AVOID 14
TIPS ON LOSING WEIGHT ON KETO 20
21-DAY KETO MEAL PLAN 27
RECIPES 33
Breakfast 33
    Kale Wrapped Eggs 33
    Zucchini Keto Bread 34
    Ham Sausage Quiche 36
    Coconut Almond Breakfast 37
    Avocado Egg Muffins 39
    Soft-Boiled Eggs 41
    Breakfast Casserole 41
    Poblano Cheese Frittata 43
    Poached Egg 44
    Spinach Egg Bites 45
    Blueberry Muffins 46
    Sous Vide Egg Bites 48
    Scrambled Eggs 49
    Taco Egg Muffins 50
    Deviled Eggs 51
    Spinach and Red Pepper Frittata 53

- Coconut Porridge 54
- Crustless Quiche Lorraine 55
- Chocolate Protein Pancakes 56
- Frittata 58
- Bacon and Zucchini Muffins 59
- Blueberry Pancake Bites 60
- Pretzels 62

Lunch 64
- Super Herbed Fish 64
- Turkey Avocado Chili 65
- Cheesy Tomato Shrimp 67
- Cajun Rosemary Chicken 69
- Chicken Spinach Curry 71
- Steamed Shrimp and Asparagus 72
- Barbecue Ribs 73
- Smothered Pork Chops 75
- Cream Cheese Stuffed Baby Peppers 76
- Artichoke Dip 77
- Taco Meat 78
- Green Beans with Bacon 79
- Beef and Broccoli 80
- Meatballs 81
- Rainbow Mason Jar Salad 83
- Fish Cakes 84
- Lasagna Stuffed Peppers 85
- Korean Ground Beef Bowl 87

Snack and Sides 89
- Asparagus Fries 89

Kale Chips 90

Guacamole 91

Zucchini Noodles 92

Cauliflower Souffle 93

Carnitas 94

Brussels Sprouts 95

Cauliflower Mashed Potatoes 96

Teriyaki Drumsticks 97

Cheesy Garlic Spaghetti Squash 98

Dinner 101

Sriracha Tuna Kabobs 101

Chicken Relleno Casserole 102

Steak Salad with Asian Spice 103

Chicken Chow Mein Stir Fry 105

Salmon with Bok-Choy 106

Whole Chicken 107

Lamb Shanks 108

Jamaican Jerk Pork Roast 110

Mexican Shredded Beef 111

Beef Stew 112

Coconut Shrimp 114

Sausage Stuffed Zucchini Boats 115

Balsamic Steaks 117

Salmon 118

Sweet and Spicy Barbecue Chicken Wings 119

Coconut Chicken 121

Buffalo Chicken Meatballs 122

Tomatillo Chili 123

Garlic Chicken 124

Soups & Stews 126

Cream Zucchini Soup 126

Coconut Chicken Soup 127

Chicken Bacon Soup 129

Cream Pepper Stew 130

Ham Asparagus Soup 132

Beef Zoodle Soup 133

Broccoli Cheese Soup 135

Zuppa Toscana 136

Thai Shrimp Soup 137

Chicken and Vegetable Soup 139

Buffalo Ranch Chicken Dip 140

Creamy Taco Soup 141

Chicken Kale Soup 142

Chicken Thigh Soup 143

Dessert 146

Almond Mug Cake 146

Tapioca Keto Pudding 147

Cream Chocolate Delight 149

Coconut Keto Pudding 150

Vanilla Cream Delight 152

Orange Custard Cups 153

Key Lime Curd 155

Thai Coconut Custard 156

Molten Brownie Cups 157

Chocolate Mousse 158

Spice Cake 160

- Coconut Almond Cake 161
- Carrot Cake 162
- Chocolate Avocado Ice Cream 163
- Mocha Mousse 165
- Strawberry Rhubarb Custard 166
- Creme Brulee 167
- Pumpkin Pie Pudding 168
- Chocolate Muffins 170
- Lemon Fat Bombs 171
- Vanilla Frozen Yogurt 172
- Ice Cream 173
- Custard 174

CONCLUSION 176
ABOUT THE AUTHOR 177

INTRODUCTION

Ketogenic diets, or keto diets, are one of the latest health and lifestyle trends that took the internet by storm. It is characterized by low carbs, medium protein, and high-fat consumption. It may sound strange and counterintuitive, but keto diets have been linked to weight loss and other mental and physical benefits to both young and old people alike.

It is no hogwash pseudoscience either because many studies have been done on the subject and they all agree that keto diets work. But how exactly do they work and how you can get started? Read more to find out.

HOW TO GET STARTED WITH THE KETOGENIC DIET?

Jumping on the keto wagon, as well as committing to anything, can be an intimidating endeavor. However, getting started with this is relatively simple. No matter how many forms of the keto diet that are out there, they share some similarities:

Restrict Carbohydrates: This is the entire point of a keto diet – little carbs intake. A keto diet should have less than 20g of net carbs a day, although some people can go up to 30g. If you can get this right, then you are well on your way to become successful in your ketogenic diet adventure. Other than that, there are a few more things to keep in mind:

1. Limit protein intake: A keto diet consists mostly of fat, not carbs or protein. Too much protein can put undue stress on your kidneys and the excess will be converted to glucose, then stored as fat anyway. So make sure that you get your protein portion just right as well. This should be the second priority after setting your daily carbs limit.
2. Use fat as a lever: Fat isn't necessarily a bad thing, especially in a keto diet because fat makes up a huge portion of your keto diet. This is because fat is both a source of energy and

satiety. Here, fat serves as a lever in your keto diet whereas carbs and protein remain constant. That means you can determine how much weight you want to gain or lose based on how much fat you consume. Because our goal is to lose weight, that means you need to eat just enough fat. No more, no less.
3. Drink water: Water is very important in a keto diet because your body needs it to store glycogen in the liver. When you eat foods low in carbs, the body uses up glycogen so you can burn fat, which also means depleting your water store as well. That means you will become dehydrated faster. You normally need 2 gallons a day, but I recommend going up to 3 or 4 gallons a day when you are on a keto diet.
4. Take care of the electrolytes: Potassium, sodium, and magnesium are the major electrolytes in the body. Since a keto diet uses up water in the body, that also means that the electrolytes go along with the water. When you do not have enough electrolytes in the body, you feel sick. This is commonly referred to as the "keto flu". Although this is only temporary, you do not have to suffer the keto fly if you keep your electrolytes level at a sufficient level. That means salting your food, drinking bone broth or any other broth, and eating picked veggies. If any of these alternatives are unfavorable for you, you can also take supplements to top up your electrolytes store, but make sure you consult your doctor first before you do that.
5. Eat when you are hungry: Only when you are hungry, then eat. Some people have the mindset that they need to eat at least 4 to 6 meals, or even snack constantly between mealtimes. No wonder why they gain weight so much. In a keto diet, frequent eating is not recommended as it can interfere with your weight loss effort. So eat only when you are hungry. If you do not feel hungry, then don't eat. But this should be easy considering that a keto diet or any other low-carb diets lack carbohydrate so this diet naturally suppresses appetite altogether.
6. Focus on whole foods: You do not have to resort to eating only natural or whole food so you can get your carbs limit down properly. However, keep in mind that processed food

is rich in carbs and will not help you get rid of cravings, not to mention that they are unhealthy in the first place.
7. Exercise: This is optional, but you should take care of your muscles at your age as they start to degrade. You will feel better, your health will improve, and your weight will go down faster.

Keto Macro

If you really want to get it down, you will need an online calculator to help you determine how much you need to eat. It is impossible to give you a direct formula because there are many variables to take into consideration. But if you are curious, a keto diet usually contains the following:

- Fat: 60% to 75%
- Protein: 15% to 30%
- Net carbs: 5% to 10%

Fat, protein and net carbs content vary from person to person, but they all stay within this range. It is worth mentioning that the sum of all three should equal 100%. The percentage is the amount of daily calorie intake.

THE SCIENCE BEHIND KETO

Okay, so we know that a ketogenic diet is characterized by low-carb, medium-protein, and high-fat intake. The combination of these three ingredients will cause the body to go into ketosis. Ketosis is a metabolic shift in the body in a way that allows the body to burn fat rather than carbohydrates.

The carbohydrates that are consumed are converted into glucose and insulin. Here, glucose is basically sugar. Glucose is the most convenient source of energy because your body can convert it to energy easier. As such, the body prefers using that up first. Another byproduct of carbohydrates is insulin, which is a hormone produced by your pancreas. This hormone helps process glucose in your body by transporting the glucose in the body to where it is needed. When your body has enough energy, the excess glucose will be converted to adipose tissue, or fat, as a backup. Of course, that does not mean that the body uses that fat first if there are carbohydrates available.

You see, the fat in your body is considered to be the backup source of power. Therefore, in a normal situation, your body would burn carbohydrates, then fats, then proteins, in that order. As such, the body does not burn fat as effectively. Ketosis promotes weight loss by making the body prioritize burning fat, thus resulting in more fat being burned.

Many ordinary diets contain plenty of carbohydrates, which are not bad in itself. It is only bad when you take in more energy than you spend it, which means you create an energy leftover which would be converted to fat. Day by day, your weight adds up very quickly. For such a diet, glucose is the main source of energy because it contains plenty of it. However, the glucose in your body can only last you a few days. Your body will convert glucose to fat if you do not use glucose up. So when your glucose store runs dry in a few days, your body will switch to another source of energy through a biochemical process known as ketogenesis.

When this process starts, your liver starts to take the fat in your body and break it down, creating an alternative source of energy. When that happens, your ketone level goes up and your body. This is the moment when you enter ketosis.

How to Enter Ketosis

You have a few options when it comes to entering ketosis.

The most direct one is by depriving your body of carbohydrates, therefore glucose, through fasting for a long period of time. When you stop eating altogether, your body will turn to burn fat as a source of energy because it has no glucose to work with. But of course, fasting and intermittent fasting is a whole different subject on its own and we will not cover that in this book. But do remember that fasting has its caveat.

Another option is to eat less. You just have to consume less than 20 to 50 grams of your daily carbohydrate intake a day. This will depend on who is fasting. Some require fewer while some require more, perhaps even more than 50 grams. However, the bottom line is that people who are on a keto diet only consume 5% of their usual carbohydrate intake.

But whatever method you use, it all boils down to this:

1. Cut down on carbs intake to 5% of regular intake
2. Increase fat intake to 80%
3. The lack of carbs will force the body to burn fat instead
4. When the ketone level in your blood rises high enough, you enter a state of ketosis
5. Profit.

Benefits

Keto diet is unlike any other diet that disappears just as abruptly as they appear. In fact, the keto diet has been practiced for far longer than you think. Its root can be traced back to the 1920s. A ketogenic diet is based on a solid understanding of physiology and nutrition science, so it is not some hogwash pseudoscience either. It is grounded on science and it has been proven to be effective.

Keto diet is very effective for many people because it provides a wide variety of benefits that anyone can benefit from, regardless of their gender or age. Some of the benefits are the direct remedy to weight gain such as hormonal imbalance (especially for menopause), elevated insulin as well as high blood sugar level. A keto diet is not only beneficial for the body either. The diet has therapeutic benefits that really help those who have brain disorders.

Weight Loss

Of course, the main reason why people jump on the keto wagon in the first place is the fact that the keto diet is an effective way to lose weight. A diet that is rich in fat content but low in carbs such as the keto diet minimizes hunger in your body. It just does not feel as hungry when you are in ketosis. Not only that, but your body's ability to burn fat is also boosted due to hormonal changes in your body.

When you eat normally by following an ordinary diet, the food you eat provides your body with carbohydrates. When they enter the system, your body releases insulin. Insulin helps regulate blood sugar levels by converting the excess into fat for later use. With a lower level of insulin, our body is more likely to use existing fat in the body for energy instead of storing the excess energy as fat.

Moreover, a keto diet that packs a lot of healthy fat and protein is very filling, which can help suppress your appetite and prevent overeating.

Cholesterol and Blood Pressure

Diabetes and high blood pressure are some of the most common reasons that result in death among older adults. Keto diet is effective in this regard because it improves triglyceride and cholesterol levels that are associated with arterial buildups. It also leads to an increase in high-density lipoprotein (HDL) and decreases in low-density lipoprotein (LDL) particles. All of this comes together to the improvement in blood pressure.

But high blood pressure can also result from cholesterol in the body, which is a consequence of excess weight.

Regulate Blood Sugar

Keto diet helps regulate blood sugar by controlling how much insulin is in the system. Maintaining the right level of insulin is important because you can avoid problems such as insulin resistance or pre-diabetes. Keto diet has also been shown to reduce HbA1c levels, which is a measure of blood glucose control.

Because the keto diet is effective at regulating insulin, therefore blood sugar level, it has an added benefit of helping people with type 2 diabetes. It may not cure them outright, but it can work in conjunction with diabetes medication or reduce its dependence.

Fights Neurological Disorders

Keto diet has been used in the past to treat neurological disorders or other cognitive impairments such as epilepsy. When your body goes into ketosis, your body produces ketones that help reverse neurodegenerative illnesses. Here, the brain just uses another source of energy instead of using the cellular energy pathway that is faulty in people with brain disorders. That means the keto diet can help prevent or treat disorders such as Parkinson's and Alzheimer's.

BEST FOODS TO FIT INTO THE KETO DIET

In this chapter, I will go over what food you should consider incorporating into your keto diet. But the general guideline is that all foods that are nutritious and low in carbs are excellent options.

Seafood

Fishes and shellfishes are perfect for keto diets. Many fishes are rich in B vitamins, potassium, as well as selenium. Salmon, sardines, mackerel, and other fatty fish also pack a lot of omega-3 fats that help in regulating insulin levels. These are so low in carbs that it is negligible.

Shellfishes are a different story because some contain very few carbs whereas others pack plenty. Shrimps and most crabs are okay but beware of other types of shellfish.

Vegetables

Most vegetables pack a lot of nutrients that your body can greatly benefit from even though they are low in calories and carbs. Plus, some of them contain fiber, which helps with your bowel movement. Moreover, your body spends more energy breaking down and digesting food rich in fiber, so it helps with weight loss as well.

Cheese

Milk, as I will discuss in the next chapter, is not okay. You can get away with cheese though. Cheese is delicious and nutritious. Thankfully, although there are hundreds of types of cheese out there, all of them are low in carbs and full of fat. Eating cheese may even help your muscles and slow down aging.

Avocados

Avocados are so famous nowadays in the health community that people associate the word "health" to avocados. This is for a very good reason because avocados are very healthy. They pack lots of vitamins and minerals such as potassium. Moreover, avocados are shown to help the body go into ketosis faster.

Meat and Poultry

These two are the staple food in most keto diets. Most of the keto meals revolve around using these two ingredients. This is because they contain no carbs and pack plenty of vitamins and minerals. Moreover, they are a great source of protein.

Eggs

Eggs form the bulk of most food you will eat in a keto diet because they are the healthiest and most versatile food item of them all. Even a large egg contains so little carbs but packs plenty of protein, making it a perfect option for a keto diet.

Moreover, eggs are shown to have an appetite suppression effect, making you feel full for longer as well as regulating blood sugar levels. This leads to lower calorie intake for about a day. Just make sure to eat the entire egg because the nutrients are in the yolk.

Coconut Oil

Coconut oil and other coconut-related products such as coconut milk and coconut powder are perfect for a keto diet. Coconut oil, especially, contain MCTs that are converted into ketones by the liver to be used as an immediate source of energy.

Plain Greek Yogurt and Cottage Cheese

These two food items are rich in protein and a small number of carbs, small enough that you can safely include them into your keto diet. They also help suppress your appetite by making you feel full for longer and they can be eaten alone and are still delicious.

Olive Oil

Olive oil is very beneficial for your heart because it contains oleic acid that helps decrease heart disease risk factors. Extra-virgin olive oil is also rich in antioxidants. The best thing is that olive oil can be used as a main source of fat and it has no carbs. The same goes for olive.

Nuts and Seeds

These are also low in carbs but rich in fat. They are also healthy and have a lot of nutrients and fiber. They help reduce heart disease, cancer, depression, and other risks of diseases. The fiber in these also help make you feel full for longer, so you would consume fewer calories and your body would spend more calories digesting them.

Berries

Many fruits pack too many carbs that make them unsuitable in a keto diet, but not berries. They are low in carbs and high in fiber. Some of the best berries to include in your diet are blackberries, blueberries, raspberries, and strawberries.

Butter and Cream

These two food items pack plenty of fat and a very small amount of carbs, making them a good option to include in your keto diet.

Shirataki Noodles

If you love noodles and pasta but don't want to give up on them, then shirataki noodles are the perfect alternative. They are rich in water content and pack a lot of fiber, so that means low carbs and calories and hunger suppression.

Unsweetened Coffee and Tea

These two drinks are carb-free, so long as you don't add sugar, milk, or any other sweeteners. Both contain caffeine that improves your metabolism and suppresses your appetite. A word of warning to those who love light coffee and tea lattes, though. They are made with non-fat milk and contain a lot of carbs.

Dark Chocolate and Cocoa Powder

These two food items are delicious and contain antioxidants. Dark chocolate is associated with the reduction of heart disease risk by lowering the blood pressure. Just make sure that you choose only dark chocolate with at least 70% cocoa solids.

FOOD TO AVOID

In this chapter, I will show you the kinds of food you want to avoid at all costs. Because keto is a keto diet, that means you need to avoid high-carbs food. Some of the food you avoid is even healthy, but they just contain too many carbs. Here is a list of common food you should limit or avoid altogether.

Bread and Grains

Breads are a staple food in many countries. You have loaves, bagels, tortillas, the list goes on. However, no matter what form bread takes, they still pack a lot of carbs. The same applies to wholegrain as well because they are made from refined flour.

Depending on your daily carb limit, eating a sandwich or bagel can put you way over your daily limit. So if you really want to eat bread, it is best to make keto variants at home instead.

Grains such as rice, wheat, and oats pack a lot of carbs as well. So limit or avoid that as well.

Fruits

Fruits are healthy for you. In fact, they have been linked to a lower risk of heart disease and cancer. However, there are a few that you need to avoid in your keto diets. The problem is that some of those foods pack quite a lot of carbs such as banana, raisins, dates, mango, and pear.

As a general rule, avoid sweet and dried fruits. Berries are an exception because they do not contain as much sugar and are rich in fiber. So you can still eat some of them, around 50 grams.

Vegetables

Vegetables are just as healthy for your body. Most of the keto diet does not care how many vegetables you eat so long as they are low in starch. Vegetables that are rich in fiber can help with weight loss. For one, they make you feel full for longer so they help suppress your appetite. Another benefit is that your body would burn more calories to break and digest them. Moreover, they help control blood sugar and aid with your bowel movements.

But that also means you need to avoid or limit vegetables that are high in starch because they have more carbs than fiber. That includes corn, potato, sweet potato, and beets.

Pasta

Pasta is also a staple food in many countries. It is versatile and convenient. As with any other convenient food, pasta is rich in carbs. So when you are on your keto diet, spaghetti or any other types of pasta are not recommended. You can probably get away with it by eating a small portion, but that is not possible.

Thankfully, that does not mean you need to give up on it altogether. If you are craving pasta, you can try some other alternatives that are low in carbs such as spiralized veggies or shirataki noodles.

Cereal

Cereal is also a huge offender because sugary breakfast cereals pack a lot of carbs. That also applies to "healthy cereals". Just because they use other words to describe their product does not mean that you should believe them. That also applies to oatmeal, whole-grain cereals, etc.

So when you eat a bowl of cereal when you are doing keto, you are already way over your carb limit, and we haven't even added milk into the equation! Therefore, avoid whole-grain cereal or cereals that we mention here altogether.

Beer

In reality, you can drink most alcoholic beverages in moderation without fear. For instance, dry wine does not have that many carbs and hard liquor has no carbs at all. So you can drink them without worry. Beer is an exception to this rule because it packs a lot of carbs.

Carbs in beers or other liquid are considered to be liquid carbs and they are even more dangerous than solid carbs. You see, when you eat food that is rich in carbs, you at least feel full. When you drink liquid carbs, you do not feel full as quickly so the appetite suppression effect is little.

Sweetened Yogurt

Yogurt is actually very healthy because it is tasty and does not have that many carbs. It is a very versatile food to have in your keto diet. The problem comes when you consume yogurt variants that are rich in carbs such as fruit-flavored, low-fat, sweetened, or nonfat yogurt. A single serving of sweetened yogurt actually contains as many carbs as a single serving of dessert.

If you really love yogurt, you can get away with half a cup of plain Greek yogurt with 50 grams of raspberries or blackberries.

Juice

Fruit juices are perhaps the worst beverage you can put into your system when you are on a keto diet. One may argue that juice provides some nutrients, but the problem is that it contains a lot of carbs that are very easy to digest. As a result, your blood sugar level will spike whenever you drink it. That also applies to vegetable juice because of the fast-digesting carbs present.

Another problem is that the brain does not process liquid carbs the same way as solid carbs. Solid carbs can help suppress appetite, but liquid carbs will only put your appetite into overdrive.

Low-fat and fat-free salad dressings

As mentioned previously, fruits and vegetables are largely okay so long as they are low in carbs. But if you have to buy salads, keep in mind that commercial dressings actually pack more carbs than you think, especially the fat-free and low-fat variants.

So if you want to enjoy your salad, dress your salad using creamy, full-fat dressing instead. To really cut down on carbs, you can use vinegar and olive oil, both of which are proven to help with heart health and aid in weight loss.

Beans and Legumes

These are also very nutritious as they are rich in fiber. Research has shown that eating these have many health benefits such as reduced inflammation and heart disease risk.

However, they are also rich in carbs. You may be able to enjoy a small amount of them when you are on your keto diet, but make sure you know exactly how much you can eat before you exceed your carb limit.

Sugar

We mean sugar in any form, including honey. You may already be aware of what foods that contain lots of sugar such as cookies, candies, and cake are forbidden on a keto diet or any other form of diet that is designed to lose weight.

What you may not be aware of is that nature's sugar such as honey is just as rich in carbs as processed sugar. In fact, natural forms of sugar contain even more carbs.

Not only that sugar, in general, is rich in carbs, they also add little to no nutritional value to your meal. When you are on a keto diet, you need to keep in mind that your diet is going to consist of food that is rich in fiber and nutritious. So sugar is out of the question.

If you really want to sweeten your food you can just use a healthy sweetener instead because they do not add as many carbs to your food.

Chips and Crackers

These two are some of the most popular snacks. What some people did not realize is that one packet of chips contain several servings and should not be all eaten in one go. The carbs can add up very quickly if you do not watch what you eat.

Crackers also pack a lot of carbs, although the amount varies based on how they are made. But even whole-wheat crackers contain a lot of carbs.

Due to how processed snacks are produced, it is difficult to stop yourself from eating everything within a short period of time. Therefore, it is advised that you avoid them altogether.

Milk

I mentioned previously that cereal contains a lot of carbs and a breakfast cereal will put you way over your carbs limit without you adding milk. Milk also contains a lot of carbs on its own. Therefore, avoid it if you can even though milk is a good source of many nutrients such as calcium, potassium, and other B vitamins.

Of course, that does not mean that you have to ditch milk altogether. You can get away with a tablespoon or two of milk for your coffee. But cream or half-and-half is better if you drink coffee frequently. These two contain very few carbs. But if you love to drink milk in large amounts or need it to make your favorite drinks, consider using coconut milk or unsweetened almond instead.

Gluten-free baked goods

Wheat, barley, and rye all contain gluten. Some people who have celiac disease still want to enjoy these delicacies but unable to because their gut will become inflamed in response to gluten. As such, gluten-free variants have been created to cater to their needs.

Gluten-free diets are very popular nowadays, but what many people don't seem to realize is that they pack quite a lot of carbs. That includes gluten-free bread, muffins, and other baked products. In reality, they contain even more carbs than their glutenous variant. Moreover, the flour used to make these gluten-free products are made from grains and starches. So when you consume a gluten-free bread, your blood sugar level spikes.

So, just stick to whole foods. Alternatively, you can use almond or coconut flour to make your own low-carb bread.

TIPS ON LOSING WEIGHT ON KETO

In this chapter, I will go over a few more things you can do so you can optimize your weight loss.

Exercise

In the fitness world, it is already established that 80% of your weight loss success comes from the diet. So just by following the keto diet alone, you are already making great progress. However, if you want that extra edge in your weight loss, consider doing exercises.

You have plenty of options here. You can do cardio exercises such as jogging, running or cycling every morning for 30 minutes, but strength training works just as well. In fact, you should do both if you can.

How much exercise should you do? It depends on how much you can handle. No point in pushing beyond the limit and regret it later, right?

Team Up

A group activity is always more entertaining. So if you can find like-minded individuals who are also into keto diets, consider doing it together with them. It makes things much easier. This tip also applies to some other tips that I will show you, such as exercise that I just covered.

Move More

Moving more here does not mean more cardio exercises. You cannot expect to get any more effective weight loss if you exercise for 30mns a day and then sit on the couch for the rest of the day. The idea is to burn more calories than you can take in, so it pays to be a little extra active throughout the day.

If you have a desk job, consider getting up at least once an hour and take a short break by walking in the lobby for at least 5 minutes. It doesn't seem much, but it helps in the long run.

Talk to a Dietitian

The first thing you should do before getting into any diet is to consult your dietitian. While the keto diet works for many people, you never really know if it will work for you. Therefore, it is wise to ask your dietitian first before you jump in, rather than suffer some adverse effects because your body is not compatible with this diet.

Cook at Home More

Or eat out less frequently. There are two reasons why you should do that. For one, there are only a few places, if at all, that serve keto-based foods, let alone those that follow your diet plan. You need to prepare your own food if you want to do a keto diet. Another benefit is economics. You will buy most of your ingredients and prepare your meals ahead of time. This means you will only spend your money on the ingredients you know you will need.

Eat More Produce

While we are on the subject of eating, consider incorporating more produces in your diet, some of which I have covered already. Vegetables and fruits are full of nutrients that your body needs to remain healthy, so it should be included in your diet.

Hire a Personal Trainer

While we are still discussing exercising, consider getting yourself a personal trainer. That way, you can get the most out of your exercises and your trainer also doubles as an exercise partner as well because they hold you accountable for your own commitments. Your trainer is very helpful when you do strength training because they can teach you how to perform the exercise with the correct form and preventing you from injuring yourself.

Rely Less on Convenience Foods

Convenient foods are convenient, but not healthy. Not by a long shot. They are rich in calories and often do not pack essential nutrients such as protein, fiber, vitamins, etc. If you can, ditch convenient foods altogether.

Find an Activity You Enjoy

When you have done enough exercise, you will know what activities you like. One way to encourage yourself to exercise more regularly is by making it entertaining than a chore. If possible, stick to your favorite activities and you can get the most out of your exercises. Keep in mind that the activities you enjoy may not be effective or needed, so you need to find other exercises to compensate, which you may not enjoy so much. For instance, if you like jogging, then you can really work your leg muscles, but your arms are not involved. So you need to do pushups or other strength training exercises.

Here, your trainer can help you decide and create a workout routine that you can stick with as well.

Check with a Healthcare Provider

As mentioned earlier, the keto diet works for many people, but it isn't for everyone. Your dietitian can tell you whether keto diet would work, but it helps to check in with your healthcare provider to ensure that you do not have any medical condition that prevents you from losing weight, such as hypothyroidism and polycystic ovarian syndrome. It helps to know well in advance whether your body is even capable of losing fat in the first place before you commit and see no result, right?

Eat Less at Night

While the science still argues about it to this day, it seems more logical that breakfast is the most important meal of the day considering that you would not have eaten for the past 8 hours whereas the interval between breakfast and lunch, and lunch and dinner is 5 or 6 hours at best. By the same token, dinner should be small because your body does not need to expend that much energy when you are sleeping anyway. So the excess energy becomes fat.

So keep dinner light. For one, it helps you lose weight. Another reason is if you have a heavy dinner, your body will strain itself trying to digest everything. That means your body would remain active until all the food is digested, meaning that you will not get restful sleep if you can sleep at all.

Bottom line: Eat light and eat dinner at least 4 hours prior to bedtime. Any sooner and you will have a hard time sleeping.

Body Composition

Your body isn't just "weight" alone. Your body is composed of fat, muscles, fluid, bones, etc. What you want to lose is fat weight, not muscle weight or fluid weight. You want as little fat mass in your body as possible while still maintaining a healthy level of non-fat mass in your body. There are many ways you can measure your body fat, but the simplest method is to measure your calves, thighs, waist, chest, and biceps.

Hydrate Properly

That means drinking enough water or herbal tea and ditch sweetened beverages or other drinks that contain sugar altogether. Making the transition will be difficult for the first few weeks, but your body will be thanking you for it. There is nothing healthier than good old plain water and the recommended amount is 2 gallons a day. However, because you are on a keto diet, your body needs to use up more water so consider 2 gallons to the absolute minimum amount of water you need to drinks. I recommend you drink between 3 or even 4 gallons a day when you are on a keto diet. If you get thirsty, then it is a sign of dehydration, so drink some water. Drinking plenty of water also leads to additional calories burned. You can shave off a few more calories by drinking cold water because your body will spend more energy trying to regulate your body temperature.

Get Enough Sleep

Getting enough sleep helps your body regulate the hormones in your body, so try to aim for 7 to 9 hours of sleep a day. You can get more restful sleep by creating a nighttime routine that involves not looking at a computer, phone, or TV screen for at least 1 hour before bed. You can drink warm milk or water to help your body relax, or even do 10 to 20 minutes of stretching so you can get a restful sleep.

While we are on the subject of sleeping, try to maintain a consistent sleeping schedule. I understand that you want to sleep and wake up 1 to 4 hours later than usual during the weekend. But you want to go to bed and wake up at the same time, your mood and energy level will be higher. An added benefit is that your body will learn to wake up on its own even without the alarm.

Mindful Eating

Mindfulness isn't restricted to meditation alone. Again, we will not go over meditation in this book because it is another topic altogether. But what you can do here is learn to love and appreciate your food. It sounds obnoxious, but it helps your mood and promotes weight loss.

Simply put, you just have to put away your phone and take away any other sources of distractions and focus solely on your food, how it tastes, etc. That means eating slowly. You will learn to appreciate how tasty your food is because you actually focus on eating.

How does this translate to weight loss? You see, there is a system in your body that determines how full you are. The issue here is that this system is not instantaneous. It takes some time to measure how full your stomach it before sending the signal to your brain. So when you eat too quickly, by the time you feel full, you would have already overshot by a country mile. If you eat slowly, your body has enough time to register your fullness bite by bite. So when you feel full, you have not overeaten.

Use Inconvenience to Your Advantage

In the last chapter, I pointed out that eating chips, crackers, or any other salty snacks can cause you to overeat very quickly. The problem is that just ditching these delicious snacks cold turkey style is difficult, especially if you have developed a taste for them. So what do you do? Well, you remove such food from your house immediately. Only have enough food in the house for the week or have only healthy snacks in the house.

Even when you have a sudden craving for unhealthy snacks, the inconvenience of going out to buy one is enough to dissuade you and help you suppress the hunger. Another solution is to tell yourself that you will grab that unhealthy snack "tomorrow". We are all professional procrastinators or were one at a certain point in our lives, so use that to your advantage as well. When you set a "plan" like that, your mind is tricked into thinking that you will get around to it when the time is right, although that time will never come.

But what if you need to go out and get groceries for next week's keto meals? You have two options.

You can go to the grocery store carrying just enough money to get everything you need for next week's meals. That way, you simply cannot afford to buy extra snacks. But this requires your prior knowledge of the prices of the products you need to buy, and any price changes can leave you with some extra change or you not having enough money. To remedy this problem, I recommend you bring a bit extra just in case there are any price changes.

An alternative that I like is to bring someone along with you for the trip, but you let them carry all the money. The amount does not matter here, but it requires the other person to be firm about not letting you buy that potato chip. They have the money and they will have to stick to the plan of buying enough for the week, nothing more than that. It is going to be a bit inconvenient for the other person, but they can hold you accountable and keep you in control of the situation.

21-DAY KETO MEAL PLAN

In this chapter, I will give you a 21-day keto meal plan so you know exactly what you need to eat for each day.

	Breakfast	Lunch	Dinner	Nutritional Values
Day 1	Avocado Bun Breakfast Burger	Avocado Cream and Zoodles	Chicken Cutlet and Cauli Rice	Calories: 1765 Fat: 139.05g Protein:90.91g Net carbs: 20.75g
Day 2	Breakfast Sausage, Eggs & Greens	Chicken Cutlet & Cauli Rice	Shirataki Noodles Asian Salad	Calories: 1374 Fat: 93g Protein: 98.61g Net Carbs: 19.79g

KETO DIET FOR BEGINNERS 2023

Day 3	Breakfast Sausage & Eggs	BLT Lettuce Boats	Grilled Cod & Shrimps	Calories: 1177 Fat: 78.94g Protein: 94.65g Net Carbs: 15.74g
Day 4	90-sec Sausage Egg Muffin	Grilled Cod & Shrimps	Arugula Caesar Salad & Veggies	Calories: 1316 Fat: 89g Net Carbs: 19.75g Protein: 99.06g
Day 5	Breakfast Sausage & Poached Egg	Rosemary Chicken & Broccoli	Rosemary Pork Roast Side Caesar Salad	Calories: 1495 Fat: 111.31g Net Carbs: 12.34g Protein: 101.2g
Day 6	Spinach & Breakfast Sausage Omelet	Rosemary Pork Roast Side Caesar Salad 2	Broccoli, Bacon & Mushrooms	Calories: 1313 Fat: 99.55g Protein: 84.98g Net carbs: 13.02g
Day 7	Spinach & Pork Omelet	Zucchini Salad with Grilled Chicken	Rosemary Pork Roast Side Caesar	Calories: 1509 Fat: 114.98g Protein: 96.37g

		Thigh	Salad	Net carbs: 15.62g
Day 8	Chorizo Breakfast Bake	Sesame Pork Lettuce Wraps	Avocado Lime Salmon	Calories: 1,520 Fat: 109g Protein: 110g Net Carbs: 16g
Day 9	Chorizo Breakfast Bake with 3 Slices Thick-Cut Bacon	Spiced Pumpkin Soup	Avocado Lime Salmon	Calories: 1,570 Fat: 124g Protein: 92g Net Carbs: 16
Day 10	Baked Eggs in Avocado	Easy Beef Curry	Easy Beef Curry	Calories: 1,700 Fat: 128.5g Protein: 103g Net Carbs: 22g
Day 11	Lemon Poppy Ricotta Pancakes with 3 Slices Thick-Cut	Spiced Pumpkin Soup with ½ Medium Avocado	Rosemary Roasted Chicken and Veggies	Calories: 1,665 Fat: 130g Protein: 95.5g Net Carbs: 23.5g

	Bacon			
Day 12	Lemon Poppy Ricotta Pancakes with 3 Slices Thick-Cut Bacon	Spiced Pumpkin Soup	Cheesy Sausage Mushroom Skillet with 1 Slice Thick-Cut Bacon	Calories: 1,650 Fat: 126g Protein: 100.5g Net Carbs: 22.5g
Day 13	Sweet Blueberry Coconut Porridge with 1 Slice Thick-Cut Bacon	Easy Beef Curry	Cheesy Sausage Mushroom Skillet	Calories: 1,670 Fat: 112g Protein: 100g Net Carbs: 33.5g
Day 14	Sweet Blueberry Coconut Porridge	Easy Beef Curry	Lamb Chops with Rosemary and Garlic	Calories: 1,625 Fat: 108g Protein: 110.5g Net Carbs: 27g
Day 15	Pepper Jack Sausage Egg Muffins with	Cabbage and Sausage Skillet with 1 Slice Thick-Cut Bacon	Gyro Salad with Avo-Tzatziki	Calories: 1,605 Fat: 118.5g Protein: 102g Net Carbs:

		½ Medium Avocado			22.5g
Day 16	Fat-Busting Vanilla Protein Smoothie	Easy Cheeseburger Salad	Chicken Zoodle Alfredo		Calories: 1,530 Fat: 113.5g Protein: 107.5g Net Carbs: 18.5g
Day 17	Pepper Jack Sausage Egg Muffins with 1 Slice Thick-Cut Bacon	Pan-Fried Pepperoni Pizza	Gyro Salad with Avo-Tzatziki		Calories: 1,650 Fat: 127.5g Protein: 101g Net Carbs: 29g
Day 18	Savory Ham and Cheese Waffles with 2 Slices Thick-Cut Bacon	Pan-Fried Pepperoni Pizzas	Cabbage and Sausage Skillet		Calories: 1,670 Fat: 129g Protein: 103g Net Carbs: 20.5g
Day 19	Savory Ham and Cheese	Cabbage and Sausage Skillet	Chicken Zoodle Alfredo		Calories: 1,620 Fat: 119g

	Waffles with 1 Slice Thick-Cut Bacon			Protein: 119g Net Carbs: 18.5g
Day 20	Mozzarella Veggie-Loaded Quiche with 1 Slice Thick-Cut Bacon	Easy Cheeseburger Salad	Gyro Salad with Avo-Tzatziki	Calories: 1,580 Fat: 104.5g Protein: 117.5g Net Carbs: 33g
Day 21	Pepper Jack Sausage Egg Muffins with 3 Slices Thick-Cut Bacon	Pan-Fried Pepperoni Pizza	Cabbage and Sausage Skillet	Calories: 1,650 Fat: 127.5g Protein: 101g Net Carbs: 29g

Keep in mind that this meal plan is not for everyone because of allergies or other medical complications, so at least consult your doctor and see what food you cannot eat and customize accordingly. So long as you know how much carbs, fat, and protein you need to consume, you are good to go.

RECIPES

Breakfast

Kale Wrapped Eggs

Prep Time: 8-10 min.

Cooking Time: 5 min.

Number of Servings: 4

Ingredients:

- Three tablespoons heavy cream
- Four hardboiled eggs
- ¼ teaspoon pepper
- Four kale leaves
- Four prosciutto slices
- ¼ teaspoon salt
- 1 ½ cups water

Directions:

1. Peel the eggs and wrap each with the kale. Wrap them in the prosciutto slices and sprinkle with ground black pepper and salt.

2. Arrange Instant Pot over a dry platform in your kitchen. Open its top lid and switch it on.
3. In the pot, pour water. Arrange a trivet or steamer basket inside that came with Instant Pot. Now place/arrange the eggs over the trivet/basket.
4. Close the lid to create a locked chamber; make sure that safety valve is in locking position.
5. Find and press "MANUAL" cooking function; timer to 5 minutes with default "HIGH" pressure mode.
6. Allow the pressure to build to cook the ingredients.
7. After cooking time is over press "CANCEL" setting. Find and press "QPR" cooking function. This setting is for quick release of inside pressure.
8. Slowly open the lid, take out the cooked recipe in serving plates or serving bowls, and enjoy the keto recipe.

Nutritional Values (Per Serving):

Calories – 247; Fat – 20g; Saturated Fat – 6g ; Trans Fat – 0g; Carbohydrates – 7g; Fiber – 3g; Sodium – 742mg; Protein – 19g.

Zucchini Keto Bread

Prep Time: 8-10 min.

Cooking Time: 40 min.

Number of Servings: 12-16 slices

Ingredients:

- 1 cup grated zucchini

- 2 ½ cups almond flour
- ½ cup chopped walnuts
- 3 eggs
- ½ cup olive oil
- 1 ½ teaspoon baking powder
- Pinch of ginger powder
- 1 teaspoon vanilla extract
- ½ teaspoon cinnamon
- ¼ teaspoon nutmeg
- pinch of sea salt
- 1 ½ cups water

Directions:

1. Whisk together the wet ingredients in a bowl.
2. Combine the dry ingredients in another bowl. Combine the dry and wet mixture. Stir in the zucchini.
3. Grease a loaf pan with some butter and pour the mixture. Top with chopped walnuts.
4. Arrange Instant Pot over a dry platform in your kitchen. Open its top lid and switch it on.
5. In the pot, pour water. Arrange a trivet or steamer basket inside that came with Instant Pot. Now place/arrange the loaf pan over the trivet/basket.
6. Close the lid to create a locked chamber; make sure that safety valve is in locking position.
7. Find and press "MANUAL" cooking function; timer to 40 minutes with default "HIGH" pressure mode.
8. Allow the pressure to build to cook the ingredients.
9. After cooking time is over press "CANCEL" setting. Find and press "QPR" cooking function. This setting is for quick release of inside pressure.

10. Slowly open the lid, take out the cooked bread.
11. Cooldown, slice, and serve.

Nutritional Values (Per Serving):

Calories – 164; Fat – 17g; Saturated Fat – 2g; Trans Fat – 0g; Carbohydrates – 3g; Fiber – 2g; Sodium – 94mg; Protein – 5g.

Ham Sausage Quiche

Prep Time: 8-10 min.

Cooking Time: 30 min.

Number of Servings: 4

Ingredients:

- 4 bacon slices, cooked and crumbled
- ½ cup diced ham
- 2 green onions, chopped
- ½ cup full-fat milk
- Six eggs, beaten
- 1 cup ground sausage, cooked
- 1 cup shredded cheddar cheese
- ¼ teaspoon salt
- Pinch of pepper
- 1 ½ cups water

Directions:

1. Grease a baking dish with coconut oil cooking spray.
2. Place all of the ingredients in a bowl, and stir to combine. Add this mixture to the prepared dish.
3. Arrange Instant Pot over a dry platform in your kitchen. Open its top lid and switch it on.
4. In the pot, pour water. Arrange a trivet or steamer basket inside that came with Instant Pot. Now place/arrange the dish over the trivet/basket.
5. Close the lid to create a locked chamber; make sure that safety valve is in locking position.
6. Find and press "MANUAL" cooking function; timer to 30 minutes with default "HIGH" pressure mode.
7. Allow the pressure to build to cook the ingredients.
8. After cooking time is over press "CANCEL" setting. Find and press "QPR" cooking function. This setting is for quick release of inside pressure.
9. Place the dish on the rack in your IP and close the lid. Cook on HIGH for 30 minutes release the pressure naturally, for 10 minutes.
10. Slowly open the lid, take out the cooked recipe in serving plates or serving bowls, and enjoy the keto recipe.

Nutritional Values (Per Serving):

Calories – 398; Fat – 31g; Saturated Fat – 13g; Trans Fat – 0g; Carbohydrates – 5g; Fiber – 1g; Sodium – 745mg; Protein – 26g.

Coconut Almond Breakfast

Prep Time: 8-10 min.

Cooking Time: 5 min.

Number of Servings: 2

Ingredients:

- 2 tablespoons roasted pepitas
- 1/3 cup coconut milk
- 2 tablespoon chopped almonds
- 1 tablespoon chia seeds
- 1/3 cup water
- One handful blueberries

Directions:

1. In your food processor or blender, mix the pepitas with almonds and pulse them well.
2. Arrange Instant Pot over a dry platform in your kitchen. Open its top lid and switch it on.
3. Add the chia seeds with water and coconut milk; gently stir to mix well.
4. Add the pepita mix and combine.
5. Close the lid to create a locked chamber; make sure that safety valve is in locking position.
6. Find and press "MANUAL" cooking function; timer to 5 minutes with default "HIGH" pressure mode.
7. Allow the pressure to build to cook the ingredients.
8. After cooking time is over press "CANCEL" setting. Find and press "QPR" cooking function. This setting is for quick release of inside pressure.
9. Slowly open the lid, take out the cooked recipe in serving plates or serving bowls, top with the blueberries, and enjoy the keto recipe.

Nutritional Values (Per Serving):

Calories – 148

Fat – 6g

Saturated Fat – 1g

Trans Fat – 0g

Carbohydrates – 4g

Fiber – 1.5g

Sodium – 346mg

Protein – 2g

Avocado Egg Muffins

Prep Time: 8-10 min; Cooking Time: 12 min; Servings: 4.

Ingredients:

- 1 ½ cups of coconut milk
- 2 avocados, diced
- 4 ½ ounces (grated or shredded) cheese
- ½ cup almond flour
- 5 bacon slices, cooked and crumbled
- 5 eggs, beaten
- 2 tablespoon butter
- 3 spring onions, diced
- 1 teaspoon oregano
- ¼ cup flaxseed meal
- 1 ½ tablespoon lemon juice

- 1 teaspoon minced garlic
- 1 teaspoon onion powder
- 1 teaspoon salt
- Pinch of pepper
- 1 teaspoon baking powder
- 1 ½ cups water

Directions:

1. Whisk together the wet ingredients.
2. Gradually stir in the dry ingredients; mix until turns smooth. Stir in the avocado, bacon, onions, and cheese.
3. Add the mixture into 16 muffin cups.
4. Arrange Instant Pot over a dry platform in your kitchen. Open its top lid and switch it on.
5. In the pot, pour water. Arrange a trivet or steamer basket inside that came with Instant Pot. Now place/arrange the 8 cups over the trivet/basket.
6. Close the lid to create a locked chamber; make sure that safety valve is in locking position.
7. Find and press "MANUAL" cooking function; timer to 12 minutes with default "HIGH" pressure mode.
8. Allow the pressure to build to cook the ingredients.
9. After cooking time is over press "CANCEL" setting. Find and press "QPR" cooking function. This setting is for quick release of inside pressure.
10. Slowly open the lid, take out the cooked recipe in serving plates or serving bowls, and enjoy the keto recipe.
11. Repeat the same process.

Nutritional Values (Per Serving):

Calories – 146; Fat – 11g; Saturated Fat – 3g; Trans Fat – 0g; Carbohydrates – 4g; Fiber – 2g; Sodium – 356mg; Protein – 6g

Soft-Boiled Eggs

Prep Time: 5 minutes; Cooking Time: 3 minutes; Servings: 4;

Ingredients:
- Eggs – 4
- Water – 2 cups

Directions:
- Switch on the instant pot, pour in water, insert steamer basket and place eggs in it.
- Shut the instant pot with its lid in the sealed position, then press the 'manual' button, press '+/-' to set the cooking time to 3 minutes and cook at low-pressure setting; when the pressure builds in the pot, the cooking timer will start.
- When the instant pot buzzes, press the 'keep warm' button, do a quick pressure release and open the lid.
- Fill a bowl with ice water, place eggs in it from the instant pot, and let rest for 3 minutes.
- Then peel the eggs, cut into slices, season with salt and black pepper and serve.

Nutritional Info:
Calories: 68; Fat: 4.6 g; Protein: 5.5 g; Net Carbs: 0.5 g; Fiber: 0 g;

Breakfast Casserole

Prep Time: 10 minutes; Cooking Time: 45 minutes; Servings: 6;

Ingredients:

- Salt – 1/2 teaspoon
- Avocado oil – 2 tablespoons
- Breakfast sausage – 6 ounces

- Broccoli stalks, grated – 1 1/2 cups
- Minced garlic – 1 tablespoon
- Salt – 1 teaspoon
- Ground black pepper – ½ teaspoon
- Eggs – 6
- Heavy cream – 1/4 cup
- Monterey jack cheese, grated – 1 cup
- Water – 1 cup
- Green onion sliced – 1
- California avocado, sliced – 1
- Sour cream – ¼ cup

Directions:

- Switch on the instant pot, grease the pot with oil, press the 'sauté/simmer' button, wait until the oil is hot and add the sausage and cook for 4 minutes or until the meat is no longer pink.
- Then add broccoli along with garlic, season with salt and black pepper and continue cooking for 2 minutes.
- Take a 7-inch baking dish, grease it with oil, spoon in cooked broccoli mixture and spread evenly.
- Crack the eggs in a bowl, add cream, whisk until combined, then add onion and cheese, whisk until mixed, pour the mixture over the sausage mixture and cover with aluminum foil.
- Press the 'keep warm' button, wipe the instant pot clean, pour in water, then insert trivet stand and place baking dish on it.
- Shut the instant pot with its lid in the sealed position, then press the 'manual' button, press '+/-' to set the cooking time to 35 minutes and cook at high-pressure setting; when the pressure builds in the pot, the cooking timer will start.
- When the instant pot buzzes, press the 'keep warm' button, release pressure naturally for 10 minutes, then do quick pressure release and open the lid.

- Take out the baking dish, uncover it and turn it over the plate to take out the frittata.
- Top the frittata with avocado, cut into slices and the top with sour cream.

Nutritional Info:

Calories: 351; Fat: 28.5 g; Protein: 18.6 g; Net Carbs: 3.9 g; Fiber: 2.9 g;

Poblano Cheese Frittata

Prep Time: 5 minutes; Cooking Time: 35 minutes; Servings: 4;

Ingredients:

- Eggs – 4
- Half-and-half – 1 cup
- Diced green chili – 10 ounces
- Salt – 1 teaspoon
- Ground cumin – 1/2 teaspoon
- Mexican cheese blend, shredded, divided – 1 cup
- Chopped cilantro – 1/4 cup
- Water – 2 cups

Directions:

- Crack eggs in a bowl, add green chilies, half-and-half, and ½ cup cheese, season with salt and cumin, stir well until incorporated.
- Take a 6-inch baking dish or silicone pan, grease it with oil, pour in the egg mixture and cover with aluminum foil.

- Switch on the instant pot, pour water in it, then insert trivet stand and place baking dish on it.
- Shut the instant pot with its lid in the sealed position, then press the 'manual' button, press '+/-' to set the cooking time to 20 minutes and cook at high-pressure setting; when the pressure builds in the pot, the cooking timer will start.
- When the instant pot buzzes, press the 'keep warm' button, release pressure naturally for 10 minutes, then do a quick pressure release and open the lid.
- Meanwhile, switch on the broiler and let it preheat.
- Take out the baking dish, spread remaining cheese on top, then place it under the broiler and broil for 5 minutes or until cheese melts and the top is nicely browned.
- When done, turn the dish over a plate to take out the frittata, then cut into slices and serve.

Nutritional Info:

Calories: 257; Fat: 19 g; Protein: 14 g; Net Carbs: 5 g; Fiber: 1 g;

Poached Egg

Prep Time: 5 minutes; Cooking Time: 7 minutes; Servings: 4;

Ingredients:

- Salt – ¾ teaspoon
- Ground black pepper – ¾ teaspoon
- Water – 1 cup
- Eggs – 4

Directions:

- Take a silicone tray, grease it with avocado oil and then crack the eggs into the cups of the tray.
- Switch on the instant pot, pour water in it, insert a trivet stand and place the silicone tray on it.
- Shut the instant pot with its lid in the sealed position, then press the 'manual' button, press '+/-' to set the cooking time to 7 minutes and cook at high-pressure setting; when the pressure builds in the pot, the cooking timer will start.
- When the instant pot buzzes, press the 'keep warm' button, do a quick pressure release and open the lid.
- Check all the eggs to see if they are completely cooked; egg whites should be firm, and yolk should be slightly jiggly.
- Run a knife around each cup in the tray, then gently scoop out the egg and transfer to a serving plate.
- Season poached eggs with salt and black pepper and serve straight away.

Nutritional Info:

Calories: 72; Fat: 4.8 g; Protein: 6.3 g; Net Carbs: 0.4 g; Fiber: 0 g;

Spinach Egg Bites

Prep Time: 5 minutes; Cooking Time: 20 minutes; Servings: 7;

Ingredients:

- Eggs – 4
- Parmesan cheese, grated – 3/4 cup
- Heavy whipping cream – 1/4 cup
- Spinach, chopped – 1/4 cup
- Prosciutto, chopped – 1/2 ounce
- Ground black pepper – 1/2 teaspoon

- Salt – 1/8 teaspoon
- Water – 1 ½ cup

Directions:

- Take an egg bite mold tray having seven cups and fill the cups evenly with prosciutto and spinach.
- Crack eggs in a bowl, add remaining ingredients except for water and whisk until smooth.
- Switch on the instant pot, pour in water and place trivet stand in it.
- Pour egg mixture evenly over spinach and prosciutto, 4 tablespoons per cup or more until 3/4th filled, and then cover the pan with aluminum foil.
- Place pan on the trivet stand, shut the instant pot with its lid in the sealed position, then press the 'manual' button, press '+/-' to set the cooking time to 10 minutes and cook at high-pressure setting; when the pressure builds in the pot, the cooking timer will start.
- When the instant pot buzzes, press the 'keep warm' button, release pressure naturally for 10 minutes, then do a quick pressure release and open the lid.
- Take out the tray, uncover it and turn over the pan onto a plate to take out the egg bites.
- Serve straight away.

Nutritional Info:

Calories: 400; Fat: 29 g; Protein: 27 g; Net Carbs: 2.5 g; Fiber: 0.5 g;

Blueberry Muffins

Prep Time: 25 minutes; Cooking Time: 20 minutes; Servings: 6;

Ingredients:

- Coconut flour – ⅓ cup
- Golden flaxseed meal – 1 ½ tablespoon
- Erythritol sweetener – 4 ½ tablespoons
- Baking powder – 1 teaspoon
- Baking soda – ¼ teaspoon
- Sea salt – ⅛ teaspoon
- Almond milk, unsweetened – 1/3 cup
- Eggs, beaten – 2
- Butter, unsalted, melted – 1 ½ tablespoon
- Vanilla extract, unsweetened – 1 teaspoon
- Blueberries, fresh – 1/3 cup
- Water – 1 cup
- Heavy cream – as needed for topping

Directions:

- Place flour in a large bowl, add flaxseed, baking powder, baking soda, sweetener and salt, and mix until well combined.
- Crack eggs in another bowl, add vanilla, butter and milk and whisk until smooth.
- Gradually mix the milk mixture into flour mixture until incorporated and smooth and then fold in berries until just mixed.
- Switch on the instant pot, pour in water, insert a trivet stand and line with a 10-inch sheet of aluminum foil.
- Spoon six silicone cupcake liners with muffin batter until ¾ full, then place the cupcakes on the lined trivet stand and cover the muffins with another sheet of aluminum foil.
- Shut the instant pot with its lid in the sealed position, then press the 'manual' button, press '+/-' to set the cooking time to 20 minutes and cook at high-pressure setting; when the pressure builds in the pot, the cooking timer will start.

- When the instant pot buzzes, press the 'keep warm' button, release pressure naturally for 10 minutes, then do a quick pressure release and open the lid.
- Remove and discard the foil, lift out muffins and let cool on a wire rack for 15 minutes.
- Pipe cream on top and serve straight away.

Nutritional Info:

Calories: 130; Fat: 11 g; Protein: 3 g; Net Carbs: 1.5 g; Fiber: 2 g;

Sous Vide Egg Bites

Prep Time: 5 minutes; Cooking Time: 10 minutes; Servings: 4;

Ingredients:

- Salt – 1/2 teaspoon
- Eggs – 4
- Slices of bacon, chopped – 4
- Parmesan cheese, grated – 3/4 cup
- Cottage cheese, grated – 1/2 cup
- Heavy cream – 1/4 cup
- Water – 1 cup

Directions:

- Switch on the instant pot, press the 'sauté/simmer' button, wait until hot and add the bacon.
- Cook chopped bacon for 5 minutes or more until crispy, transfer it to a plate lined with paper towels, let rest for 5 minutes and then crumble it.

- Crack eggs in a bowl, season with salt, add cheeses and cream and blend until smooth.
- Distribute crumbled bacon evenly between the molds of a silicone tray, greased with oil, then pour in the egg mixture until 3/4th full and cover the tray loosely with foil.
- Press the 'keep warm' button, pour water in the instant pot, then insert the trivet stand and place silicone tray on it.
- Shut the instant pot with its lid in the sealed position, then press the 'steam' button, press '+/-' to set the cooking time to 8 minutes and cook at high-pressure setting; when the pressure builds in the pot, the cooking timer will start.
- When the instant pot buzzes, press the 'keep warm' button, release pressure naturally for 10 minutes, then do a quick pressure release and open the lid.
- Take out the tray, uncover it and turn over the pan onto a plate to take out the egg bites.
- Serve straight away.

Nutritional Info:

Calories: 337; Fat: 26 g; Protein: 19 g; Net Carbs: 6 g; Fiber: 0 g;

Scrambled Eggs

Prep Time: 5 minutes; Cooking Time: 7 minutes; Servings: 4;

Ingredients:

- Salt – 1/4 teaspoon
- Ground black pepper – 1/4 teaspoon
- Butter, unsalted – ½ tablespoon
- Almond milk, unsweetened, full-fat – 1 tablespoon
- Eggs – 2
- Water – 1 cup

Directions:

- Take a heatproof bowl that fits into the instant pot, grease it with avocado oil and crack eggs in it.
- Season eggs with salt and black pepper, pour in milk, whisk until blended and then add butter.
- Switch on the instant pot, pour in water, insert the trivet stand and place bowl on it.
- Shut the instant pot with its lid in the sealed position, then press the 'manual' button, press '+/-' to set the cooking time to 7 minutes and cook at low-pressure setting; when the pressure builds in the pot, the cooking timer will start.
- When the instant pot buzzes, press the 'keep warm' button, do a quick pressure release and open the lid.
- Take out the bowl, stir the eggs with a fork to check if they are cooked through; cook for another minute if eggs are undercooked.
- Serve straight away.

Nutritional Info:

Calories: 197; Fat: 15 g; Protein: 13.5 g; Net Carbs: 1 g; Fiber: 0 g;

Taco Egg Muffins

Prep Time: 10 minutes; Cooking Time: 30 minutes; Servings: 8;

Ingredients:

- Ground beef, grass-fed – ½ pound
- Taco seasoning – 1 ½ tablespoon
- Salted butter, melted – 1 tablespoon

- Eggs, organic – 3
- Mexican cheese blend, shredded and full-fat – 3 ounces
- Tomato salsa, organic – ½ cup

Directions:

- Set oven to 350 degrees F and preheat.
- Meanwhile, place a skillet pan over medium heat, grease with oil and when hot, add ground beef and cook for 7 minutes or more until almost cooked.
- Season beef with the taco seasoning and cook for 3 to 5 minutes or until cooked through, then remove the pan from heat.
- Crack eggs in a bowl, whisk until beaten, then add cooked taco beef along with 2 ounces of Mexican cheese and whisk until well combined.
- Take a 32 cups muffin pan, or parchment-lined silicone muffin cups, grease each cup with melted butter, then evenly fill with taco beef mixture and top with remaining cheese.
- Place muffin pan into the oven and bake for 20 minutes or until muffins are cooked through, and the top is nicely golden brown.
- When done, let muffins cool in the pan for 10 minutes, then take them out and cool on a wire rack.
- Serve muffins with salsa.

Nutritional Info:

Calories: 329; Fat: 22.15 g; Protein: 25.2 g; Net Carbs: 1.8 g; Fiber: 1.2 g;

Deviled Eggs

Prep Time: 15 minutes; Cooking Time: 5 minutes; Servings: 6;

Ingredients:

- Organic eggs – 12
- Salt – ½ teaspoon
- Ground black pepper – ½ teaspoon
- Smoked paprika – ½ teaspoon
- Dijon mustard – 1 tablespoon
- Mayonnaise, full-fat – ¾ cup
- Water – 1 cup

Directions:

- Switch on the instant pot, pour in water, insert steamer rack and place eggs on it.
- Shut instant pot with its lid, sealed completely, press manual button and cook eggs for 5 minutes on high pressure.
- When done, let the pressure release naturally for 5 minutes, then do a quick pressure release and open the instant pot.
- Transfer eggs into a large bowl containing ice-chilled water for 5 minutes, then peel them and cut each egg into half.
- Transfer egg yolk from each egg into a bowl, add mustard and mayonnaise, season with salt and black pepper and stir until mixed.
- Spoon the yolk filling into the egg white shells and then sprinkle with paprika.
- Serve immediately.

Nutritional Info:

Calories: 321.5; Fat: 30.1 g; Protein: 12.1 g; Net Carbs: 1 g; Fiber: 0.1 g;

Spinach and Red Pepper Frittata

Prep Time: 5 minutes; Cooking Time: 22 minutes; Servings: 8;

Ingredients:

- Eggs – 8
- Heavy whipping cream – 1/3 cup
- Shredded cheddar cheese – 1/2 cup
- Diced red bell pepper – 1/4 cup
- Minced red onion – 1/4 cup
- Chopped spinach – 1/2 cup
- Sea salt – 1 tsp
- Red chili powder – 1 tsp
- Ground black pepper – 1/8 tsp
- Water – 1 cup
- Avocado, peeled, pitted, sliced – 1
- Sour cream – 1/2 cup

Directions:

- Crack eggs in a bowl, add cream and whisk until beaten and fluffy.
- Add remaining ingredients, except for water, avocado and sour cream, stir well until incorporated and then pour the mixture in a 7-inch baking dish greased with avocado oil.
- Switch on the instant pot, pour water in it, insert a trivet stand and place baking dish on it.
- Shut the instant pot with its lid in the sealed position, then press the 'manual' button, press '+/-' to set the cooking time to 12 minutes and cook at high-pressure setting; when the pressure builds in the pot, the cooking timer will start.

- When the instant pot buzzes, press the 'keep warm' button, release pressure naturally for 10 minutes, then do a quick pressure release and open the lid.
- Take out the baking dish and take out the frittata by inverting the dish onto a plate, and cut into slices.
- Serve straight away.

Nutritional Info:

Calories: 218; Fat: 17.6 g; Protein: 9.4 g; Net Carbs: 3.5 g; Fiber: 2 g;

Coconut Porridge

Prep Time: 5 minutes; Cooking Time: 13 minutes; Servings: 6;

Ingredients:

- Shredded coconut, unsweetened – 1 cup
- Coconut milk, unsweetened and full-fat – 2 cups
- Water – 2 2/3 cups
- Coconut flour – 1/4 cup
- Psyllium husks – 1/4 cup
- Vanilla extract, unsweetened – 1 teaspoon
- Cinnamon – 1/2 teaspoon
- Nutmeg – 1/4 teaspoon
- Stevia, liquid – 30 drops
- Monk fruit sweetener, liquid – 20 drops

Directions:

- Switch on the instant pot, press the 'sauté/simmer' button, wait until hot and add the coconut and cook for 3 minutes or more until toasted.
- Pour in water and milk, stir well and press the 'keep warm' button.
- Shut the instant pot with its lid in the sealed position, then press the 'manual' button, press '+/-' to set the cooking time to 10 minutes and cook at high-pressure setting; when the pressure builds in the pot, the cooking timer will start.
- When the instant pot buzzes, press the 'keep warm' button, release pressure naturally for 10 minutes, then do a quick pressure release and open the lid.
- Add remaining ingredients, stir well and serve.

Nutritional Info:

Calories: 303; Fat: 25 g; Protein: 3 g; Net Carbs: 10 g; Fiber: 11 g;

Crustless Quiche Lorraine

Prep Time: 5 minutes; Cooking Time: 40 minutes; Servings: 4;

Ingredients:

- Slices of bacon, chopped – 8
- Eggs – 4
- Salt – ¼ teaspoon
- Nutmeg – ¼ teaspoon
- Heavy whipping cream – 1 ½ cup
- Swiss cheese, shredded – 1 1/3 cup
- Ground black pepper – ¼ teaspoon
- Water – 1 cup

Directions:

- Switch on the instant pot, press the 'sauté/simmer' button, wait until hot and add the bacon.
- Cook chopped bacon for 5 minutes or more until crispy, then transfer it to a plate lined with paper towels and set aside.
- Crack eggs in a bowl, add cream, season with salt, black pepper, and nutmeg and whisk until combined.
- Take a 6-inch baking dish, place 1 cup cheese in the bottom, then top with bacon and evenly pour in the egg mixture.
- Press the 'keep warm' button, pour water in the instant pot, insert a trivet stand and place baking dish on it.
- Shut the instant pot with its lid in the sealed position, then press the 'manual' button, press '+/-' to set the cooking time to 25 minutes and cook at high-pressure setting; when the pressure builds in the pot, the cooking timer will start.
- When the instant pot buzzes, press the 'keep warm' button, release pressure naturally for 10 minutes, then do a quick pressure release and open the lid.
- Meanwhile, switch on the broiler and let it preheat.
- Take out the baking dish, spread the remaining cheese on top, then place it under the broiler and broil for 5 minutes or until the cheese melts and the top is nicely browned.
- When done, turn the dish over a plate to take out the quiche, then cut into slices and serve.

Nutritional Info:

Calories: 572.5; Fat: 52.54 g; Protein: 22 g; Net Carbs: 3.5 g; Fiber: 0.03 g;

Chocolate Protein Pancakes

Prep Time: 10 minutes; Cooking Time: 15 minutes; Yields: 12 pancakes;

Ingredients:

- Almond flour, blanched – 1/2 cup
- Whey protein powder – 1/2 cup
- Baking powder – 1 teaspoon
- Sea salt – 1/8 tsp
- Erythritol sweetener – 3 tablespoons
- Vanilla extract, unsweetened – 1 teaspoon
- Cocoa powder, organic, unsweetened – 3 tablespoons
- Eggs, pastured – 4
- Avocado oil – 2 tablespoons
- Almond milk, unsweetened – 1/3 cup

Directions:

- Place all the ingredients in a large mixing bowl, beat using an immersion blender or until well combined and then let the mixture stand for 5 minutes.
- Then take a medium skillet pan, place it over medium-low heat, grease it with avocado oil and pour in prepared pancake batter in small circles of about 3-inches diameter.
- Cover the skillet pan with lid, let the pancakes cook for 3 minutes or until bubbles form on top, then flip them and continue cooking for 1 to 2 minutes or until nicely golden brown.
- Cook remaining pancakes, in the same manner, you will end up with 12 pancakes, and then let them cool at room temperature.
- Place cooled pancakes in a freezer bag, with parchment sheet between them and freeze them for up to 3 months or store in the refrigerator for 5 to 7 days.
- When ready to serve, and microwave pancakes for 30 seconds to 1 minute or bake in the oven for 5 minutes until thoroughly heated.

Nutritional Info:

Calories: 237; Fat: 20 g; Protein: 11 g; Net Carbs: 5 g; Fiber: 2 g;

Frittata

Prep Time: 5 minutes; Cooking Time: 17 minutes; Yield: 1 frittata;

Ingredients:

- Bacon slices, pastured, diced – 5 ounces
- Medium red onion, peeled, diced – 1/2
- Red bell pepper, cored, diced – 1/2
- Salt – 1/4 teaspoon
- Ground black pepper – 1 teaspoon
- Avocado oil – 3 tablespoons
- Grated parmesan cheese, full-fat – 1/4 cup and 2 tablespoons
- Eggs, pastured – 6

Directions:

- Take an 8 inches skillet pan, grease with oil and place it over medium heat.
- Add onion, pepper and bacon, cook for 5 minutes or until slightly golden and then season with salt and black pepper.
- Meanwhile, crack the eggs in a bowl, add ¼ cup cheese and whisk until combined.
- When bacon is cooked, pour the egg mixture into the pan, spread evenly and cook for 5 minutes or until frittata is set.
- In the meantime, switch on the broiler and let preheat.

- When the frittata is set, sprinkle remaining cheese on the top, then place the pan under the broiler and cook for 4 minutes or until golden brown.
- Let the frittata cool at room temperature, then cut it into four pieces, place each frittata piece in a heatproof glass meal prep containers and store them in the refrigerator for 5 to 7 days.
- When ready to serve, microwave frittata in their container for 1 to 2 minutes or until thoroughly heated.

Nutritional Info:

Calories: 494; Fat: 40 g; Protein: 32 g; Net Carbs: 2.9 g; Fiber: 0.1 g;

Bacon and Zucchini Muffins

Prep Time: 10 minutes; Cooking Time: 35 minutes; Yield: 8 muffins;

Ingredients:

- Grated zucchini – 2 cups
- Green onion, chopped – 1
- Thyme sprigs leaves removed – 2
- Coconut flour – 1/2 cup
- Eggs, pastured – 7
- Salt – 1/2 teaspoon
- Ground turmeric – 1 teaspoon
- Slices of bacon, pastured, diced – 5
- Baking powder – 1 teaspoon
- Apple cider vinegar – 1/2 tablespoon
- Collagen peptides – 1 scoop

Directions:

- Set oven to 350 degrees F and let preheat until muffins are ready to bake.
- Take a medium frying pan, place it over medium heat, add bacon pieces, and cook for 3 to 5 minutes until crispy.
- Then transfer cooked bacon in a large bowl, add remaining ingredients and stir until well combined.
- Take an eight cups silicon muffin tray, grease the cups with avocado oil and then evenly scoop the prepared batter in them.
- Place the muffin tray into the oven and bake the muffins for 30 minutes or until thoroughly cooked and the top is nicely golden brown.
- When done, take out muffins from the tray and cool on the wire rack.
- Place muffins in a large freezer bag or wrap each muffin with a foil and store them in the refrigerator for four days or in the freezer for up to 3 months.
- When ready to serve, microwave muffins for 45 seconds to 1 minute or until thoroughly heated.

Nutritional Info:

Calories: 104; Fat: 7.2 g; Protein: 7.9 g; Net Carbs: 1.5 g; Fiber: 0.9 g;

Blueberry Pancake Bites

Prep Time: 10 minutes; Cooking Time: 25 minutes; Yield: 24 pancake bites;

Ingredients:

- Frozen blueberries – 1/2 cup
- Coconut flour – 1/2 cup
- Baking powder – 1 teaspoon

- Salt – 1/2 teaspoon
- Swerve Sweetener – 1/4 cup
- Cinnamon – 1/4 teaspoon
- Vanilla extract, unsweetened – 1/2 teaspoon
- Butter, grass-fed, unsalted, melted – 1/4 cup
- Eggs, pastured – 4
- Water – 1/3 cup

Directions:

- Set oven to 350 degrees F and let preheat until muffins are ready to bake.
- Crack the eggs in a bowl, add vanilla and sweetener, whisk using an immersion blender until blended and then blend in salt, cinnamon, butter, baking powder, and flour until incorporated and smooth batter comes together.
- Let the batter sit for 10 minutes or until thickened and then blend in water until combined.
- Take a 25 cups silicone mini-muffin tray, grease the cups with avocado oil, then evenly scoop the prepared batter in them and top with few blueberries, pressing the berries gently into the batter.
- Place the muffin tray into the oven and bake the muffins for 25 minutes or until thoroughly cooked and the top is nicely golden brown.
- When done, take out muffins from the tray and cool them on the wire rack.
- Place muffins in a large freezer bag or evenly divide them in packets and store them in the refrigerator for four days or in the freezer for up to 3 months.
- When ready to serve, microwave the muffins for 45 seconds to 1 minute or until thoroughly heated.

Nutritional Info:

Calories: 188; Fat: 13.8 g; Protein: 5.7 g; Net Carbs: 3.8 g; Fiber: 3.7 g;

Pretzels

Prep Time: 10 minutes; Cooking Time: 12 minutes; Yield: 6 pretzels;

Ingredients:

- Almond flour, blanched – 1 1/2 cups
- Coconut sugar – 1/2 teaspoon
- Baking powder – 1 tablespoon
- Xanthan gum – 1/4 teaspoon
- Dry yeast, active – 2 1/4 teaspoon
- Water, lukewarm – 1/4 cup
- Eggs, Pastured, beaten – 2
- Mozzarella cheese, full-fat, shredded – 3 cups
- Cream cheese, full-fat, cubed – 2 ounces
- Salt – 1 teaspoon

Directions:

- Place yeast in a small bowl, add sugar, pour in water, stir until just mixed and let it sit at a warm place for 10 minutes or until frothy.
- Then pour the yeast mixture in a food processor, add flour, xanthan gums, eggs, and baking powder and pulse for 1 to 2 minutes or until well combined.
- Take a heatproof bowl, add cream cheese and mozzarella and microwave for 2 minutes or until melted, stirring every 30 seconds until smooth.
- Add melted cheese into the processed flour mixture and continue blending until the dough comes together, scraping the mixture from the sides of the blender frequently.
- Transfer the dough into a bowl and then place it in the refrigerator for 20 minutes or until chilled.

- Meanwhile, set the oven to 400 degrees F and let preheat.
- Take out the chilled dough from the refrigerator, then divide the dough into six sections and shape each section into a bowl, using oiled hands.
- Working on one section at a time, first, roll the section into an 18-inches long log, then take one end, loop it around and down across the bottom and loop the other end, in the same manner, crossing over the first loop to form a pretzel.
- Prepare remaining pretzels in the same manner and place them on a baking sheet lined with parchment sheet.
- Sprinkle salt over pretzels, pressing down lightly, then place the baking sheet into the oven and bake pretzels for 10 to 12 minutes until nicely golden.
- When done, cool the pretzels at room temperature, then keep them in a large plastic bag and store in the refrigerator for up to a week or freeze for up to 3 months.
- When ready to serve, bake the pretzels at 400 degrees F for 6 to 7 minutes until hot.

Nutritional Info:

Calories: 370; Fat: 28 g; Protein: 23 g; Net Carbs: 6 g; Fiber: 3 g;

Lunch

Super Herbed Fish

Prep Time: 8-10 min.

Cooking Time: 6 min.

Number of Servings: 1

Ingredients:

- 1 tablespoon chopped basil
- 2 teaspoons lime zest
- 1 tablespoon lime juice
- 1 tablespoon olive oil
- 1 4-ounce fish fillet
- 1 rosemary sprig
- 1 thyme sprig
- 1 teaspoon Dijon mustard
- ¼ teaspoon garlic powder
- Pinch of salt
- Pinch of pepper
- 1 ½ cups water

Directions:

1. Season the fish with salt and paper. Arrange on a piece of parchment paper and sprinkle with zest.
2. Whisk together the oil, juice, and mustard in a mixing bowl and brush over. Top with the herbs.
3. Wrap the fish with the parchment paper. Wrap the wrapped fish in an aluminum foil.

4. Arrange Instant Pot over a dry platform in your kitchen. Open its top lid and switch it on.
5. In the pot, pour water. Arrange a trivet or steamer basket inside that came with Instant Pot. Now place/arrange the foil over the trivet/basket.
6. Close the lid to create a locked chamber; make sure that safety valve is in locking position.
7. Find and press "MANUAL" cooking function; timer to 5 minutes with default "HIGH" pressure mode.
8. Allow the pressure to build to cook the ingredients.
9. After cooking time is over press "CANCEL" setting. Find and press "QPR" cooking function. This setting is for quick release of inside pressure.
10. Slowly open the lid, take out the cooked recipe in serving plates or serving bowls, and enjoy the keto recipe.

Nutritional Values (Per Serving):

Calories – 246; Fat – 9g; Saturated Fat – 1g; Trans Fat – 0g; Carbohydrates – 1g; Fiber – 0.5g; Sodium – 86mg; Protein – 28g.

Turkey Avocado Chili

Prep Time: 8-10 min.

Cooking Time: 50 min.

Number of Servings: 3-4

Ingredients:

- 2 ½ pounds lean (finely ground) turkey
- 2 cups diced tomatoes

- 2-ounce tomato paste, sugar-free
- 1 tablespoon olive oil
- ½ chopped large yellow onion
- 8 minced garlic cloves
- 1 (4-ounce) can green chilies with liquid
- 2 tablespoons Worcestershire sauce
- 1 tablespoon dried oregano
- ¼ cup red chili powder
- 2 tablespoons (finely ground) cumin
- Salt and freshly (finely ground) black pepper, as per taste preference
- 1 pitted and sliced avocado, peeled

Directions:

1. Arrange Instant Pot over a dry platform in your kitchen. Open its top lid and switch it on.
2. Find and press "SAUTE" cooking function; add the oil in it and allow it to heat.
3. In the pot, add the onions; cook (while stirring) until turns translucent and softened for around 4-5 minutes.
4. Add the garlic and cook for about 1 minute.
5. Add the turkey and cook for about 8-9 minutes. Stir in remaining ingredients except for the avocado.
6. Close the lid to create a locked chamber; make sure that safety valve is in locking position.
7. Find and press "MEAT/STEW" cooking function; timer to 35 minutes with default "HIGH" pressure mode.
8. Allow the pressure to build to cook the ingredients.
9. After cooking time is over press "CANCEL" setting. Find and press "NPR" cooking function. This setting is

for the natural release of inside pressure, and it takes around 10 minutes to release pressure slowly.
10. Slowly open the lid, take out the cooked recipe in serving plates or serving bowls, top with the avocado slices, and enjoy the keto recipe.

Nutritional Values (Per Serving):

Calories – 346; Fat – 19g; Saturated Fat – 4g; Trans Fat – 0g; Carbohydrates – 7g; Fiber – 5g; Sodium – 246mg: Protein – 29g.

Cheesy Tomato Shrimp

Prep Time: 8-10 min.

Cooking Time: 15 min.

Number of Servings: 4

Ingredients:

- 2 tablespoons olive oil
- ½ cup veggie broth
- ¼ cup chopped cilantro
- 2 tablespoons lime juice
- 1 ½ pounds shrimp, peeled and deveined
- 1 ½ pounds tomatoes, chopped
- 1 jalapeno, diced
- 1 onion, diced
- 1 cup shredded cheddar cheese
- 1 teaspoon minced garlic

Directions:

1. Arrange Instant Pot over a dry platform in your kitchen. Open its top lid and switch it on.
2. Find and press "SAUTE" cooking function; add the oil in it and allow it to heat.
3. In the pot, add the onions; cook (while stirring) until turns translucent and softened for around 2-3 minutes.
4. Add garlic and sauté for 30-60 seconds.
5. Stir in the broth, cilantro, and tomatoes.
6. Close the lid to create a locked chamber; make sure that safety valve is in locking position.
7. Find and press "MANUAL" cooking function; timer to 9 minutes with default "HIGH" pressure mode.
8. Allow the pressure to build to cook the ingredients.
9. After cooking time is over press "CANCEL" setting. Find and press "NPR" cooking function. This setting is for the natural release of inside pressure, and it takes around 10 minutes to release pressure slowly.
10. Add the shrimps.
11. Close the top lid to create a locked chamber; make sure that safety valve is in locking position.
12. Find and press "MANUAL" cooking function; timer to 2 minutes with default "HIGH" pressure mode.
13. Allow the pressure to build to cook the ingredients.
14. After cooking time is over press "CANCEL" setting. Find and press "NPR" cooking function. This setting is for the natural release of inside pressure, and it takes around 10 minutes to release pressure slowly.
15. Slowly open the lid, take out the cooked recipe in serving plates or serving bowls, top with the cheddar, and enjoy the keto recipe.

Nutritional Values (Per Serving):

Calories – 268

Fat – 16g

Saturated Fat – 5g

Trans Fat – 0g

Carbohydrates – 7g

Fiber – 2g

Sodium – 208mg

Protein – 22g

Cajun Rosemary Chicken

Prep Time: 8-10 min.

Cooking Time: 30 min.

Number of Servings: 4

Ingredients:

- 2 teaspoons Cajun seasoning
- 1 lemon, halved
- 1 yellow onion, make quarters
- 1 teaspoon garlic salt
- 1 medium chicken
- 2 rosemary sprigs
- 1 tablespoon coconut oil

- 1/4 teaspoon pepper
- 1 1/2 cups chicken broth

Directions:

1. Season the chicken with garlic salt, pepper, and Cajun seasoning. Stuff the lemon, onion, and rosemary in the chicken's cavity.
2. Arrange Instant Pot over a dry platform in your kitchen. Open its top lid and switch it on.
3. Find and press "SAUTE" cooking function; add the oil in it and allow it to heat.
4. In the pot, add the meat; cook (while stirring) until turns evenly brown from all sides.
5. Add the broth; gently stir to mix well.
6. Close the lid to create a locked chamber; make sure that safety valve is in locking position.
7. Find and press "MANUAL" cooking function; timer to 25 minutes with default "HIGH" pressure mode.
8. Allow the pressure to build to cook the ingredients.
9. After cooking time is over press "CANCEL" setting. Find and press "NPR" cooking function. This setting is for the natural release of inside pressure, and it takes around 10 minutes to release pressure slowly.
10. Slowly open the lid, take out the cooked recipe in serving plates or serving bowls, and enjoy the keto recipe.

Nutritional Values (Per Serving):

Calories – 236; Fat – 26g; Saturated Fat – 7g; Trans Fat – 0g; Carbohydrates – 1g; Fiber – 5g; Sodium – 426mg; Protein – 31g.

Chicken Spinach Curry

Prep Time: 8-10 min.

Cooking Time: 17 min.

Number of Servings: 3-4

Ingredients:

- 2 tomatoes, chopped
- 4 ounces spinach, chopped
- 1/3 pound curry paste
- 1 1/2 cups yogurt
- 4 pounds chicken, cubed
- 1 tablespoon olive oil
- 1 onion, cut to make slices
- 1 tablespoon chopped coriander

Directions:

1. Combine the chicken, curry paste, and yogurt in a mixing bowl. Cover and marinate in the fridge for 30 minutes.
2. Arrange Instant Pot over a dry platform in your kitchen. Open its top lid and switch it on.
3. Find and press "SAUTE" cooking function; add the oil in it and allow it to heat.
4. In the pot, add the onions; cook (while stirring) until turns translucent and softened.
5. Add the tomatoes and cook for another minute.

6. Pour the chicken mixture, mix in the spinach and coriander; gently stir to mix well.
7. Close the lid to create a locked chamber; make sure that safety valve is in locking position.
8. Find and press "MANUAL" cooking function; timer to 15 minutes with default "HIGH" pressure mode.
9. Allow the pressure to build to cook the ingredients.
10. After cooking time is over press "CANCEL" setting. Find and press "QPR" cooking function. This setting is for quick release of inside pressure.
11. Slowly open the lid, take out the cooked recipe in serving plates or serving bowls, and enjoy the keto recipe.

Nutritional Values (Per Serving):

Calories – 384; Fat – 18g; Saturated Fat – 3g; Trans Fat – 0g; Carbohydrates – 12g; Fiber – 6g; Sodium – 182mg; Protein – 39g.

Steamed Shrimp and Asparagus

Prep Time: 5 minutes; Cooking Time: 2 minutes; Servings: 4;

Ingredients:

- Shrimp, peeled, deveined – 1 pound
- Bunch of asparagus – 1
- Avocado oil – 1 teaspoon
- Cajun seasoning – ½ tablespoon
- Water – 1 cup
- Heavy cream – 2 cups
- Minced garlic – 3 tablespoons

Directions:

- Switch on the instant pot, pour in water, insert steel steamer rack, place asparagus on it in a single layer and then top with shrimps.
- Drizzle oil over shrimps, sprinkle with Cajun seasoning and shut the instant pot with its lid in the sealed position.
- Then press the 'steam' button, press '+/-' to set the cooking time to 2 minutes and cook at high-pressure setting; when the pressure builds in the pot, the cooking timer will start.
- Meanwhile, prepare the cream sauce and for this, whisk together garlic and cream until combined and set aside until required.
- When the instant pot buzzes, press the 'keep warm' button, do a quick pressure release and open the lid.
- Transfer shrimps and asparagus to a dish and serve with garlic cream.

Nutritional Info:

Calories: 413.9; Fat: 29.7 g; Protein: 23.8 g; Net Carbs: 7.1 g; Fiber: 5 g;

Barbecue Ribs

Prep Time: 10 minutes; Cooking Time: 40 minutes; Servings: 4;

Ingredients:

For Ribs:
- Water – 1 cup
- Apple cider vinegar – 1/4 cup
- Rack of pork spare ribs – 4 pounds
- Garlic powder – 1/2 teaspoon

- Onion powder – 1/2 teaspoon
- Salt – 2 teaspoons
- Ground black pepper – 1 teaspoon

For White Barbecue Sauce:

- Coconut milk, unsweetened and full-fat – 27 ounces
- Apple cider vinegar – 2 tablespoons
- Lemon juice – 2 tablespoons
- Mustard, whole grain – 2 tablespoons
- Minced garlic – 2 tablespoons
- Sea salt – 1 teaspoon
- Ground black pepper – 1 teaspoon
- Sriracha sauce – ½ teaspoon

Directions:

- Switch on the instant pot, place ribs in its bottom, then pour in water, drizzle with vinegar.
- Take out the ribs, pat dry with paper towels, then sprinkle with garlic and onion powder, season with salt and black pepper.
- Insert a steel steamer rack in the pot, place the rack of ribs vertically and shut the instant pot with its lid in the sealed position.
- Press the 'manual' button, press '+/-' to set the cooking time to 25 minutes and cook at high-pressure setting; when the pressure builds in the pot, the cooking timer will start.
- Meanwhile, prepare the sauce and for this, place a saucepan over medium-high heat, pour in the milk and bring it to a boil.
- Switch heat to low, simmer the milk for 15 minutes or until thickened, then remove the pan from heat, add remaining ingredients for the sauce and whisk until smooth.
- Switch on the broiler and let it preheat.
- When the instant pot buzzes, press the 'keep warm' button, release pressure naturally for 10 minutes, then do a quick pressure release and open the lid.

- Transfer ribs to a baking sheet, brush generously with prepared barbecue sauce, then place the sheet under the broiler and cook for 5 minutes or until a dark crust forms.
- When done, cut ribs into desired pieces and serve with remaining barbecue sauce.

Nutritional Info:

Calories: 766; Fat: 66 g; Protein: 36 g; Net Carbs: 4 g; Fiber: 1 g;

Smothered Pork Chops

Prep Time: 10 minutes; Cooking Time: 40 minutes; Servings: 4;

Ingredients:

- Pork loin chops, boneless – 4, each about 6-ounce
- Avocado oil – 2 tablespoons
- Medium white onion, sliced – ½
- Baby Bella mushrooms, sliced – 6 ounces
- Butter, unsalted – 1 tablespoon
- Heavy whipping cream – ½ cup
- Xanthan gum – ½ teaspoon
- Chopped parsley – 1 tablespoon
  For Spice Mix:
- Paprika – 1 tablespoon
- Garlic powder – 1 teaspoon
- Onion powder – 1 teaspoon
- Ground black pepper – 1 teaspoon
- Salt – 1 teaspoon
- Cayenne pepper – ¼ teaspoon

Directions:

- Place all the ingredients for the spice mix in a bowl, stir well, then sprinkle 1 tablespoon of the spice mix on both of the pork chops and rub well, reserving remaining spice mix.
- Switch on the instant pot, grease pot with oil, press the 'sauté/simmer' button, wait until the oil is hot and add the pork chops and cook for 3 minutes per side or until browned.
- Transfer pork chops to a plate, add onion and mushrooms, then top with browned pork chops, press the 'keep warm' button and shut the instant pot with its lid in the sealed position.
- Press the 'manual' button, press '+/-' to set the cooking time to 25 minutes and cook at high-pressure setting; when the pressure builds in the pot, the cooking timer will start.
- When the instant pot buzzes, press the 'keep warm' button, release pressure naturally for 10 minutes, then do a quick pressure release and open the lid.
- Transfer pork chops to a plate, cover with foil and set aside.
- Press the 'sauté/simmer' button, add cream and butter, whisk into the gravy in the instant pot, then whisk in ¼ teaspoon xanthan gum and simmer for 3 to 5 minutes or until the sauce starts to thicken.
- Press the 'keep warm' button, whisk in remaining xanthan gum and continue whisking until gravy reaches a desired consistency.
- Ladle gravy on pork chops, garnish with parsley and serve.

Nutritional Info:

Calories: 481.2; Fat: 32.6 g; Protein: 40 g; Net Carbs: 4 g; Fiber: 2.4 g;

Cream Cheese Stuffed Baby Peppers

Prep Time: 5 minutes; Cooking Time: 10 minutes; Servings: 4;

Ingredients:

- Organic baby peppers – 6
- Cream cheese, full-fat – 6 tablespoons

Directions:

- Rinse peppers, pat dry with paper towels, then slice the top off.
- Remove seeds from each pepper, then stuff with cream cheese until full.
- Serve immediately

Nutritional Info:

Calories: 145; Fat: 12 g; Protein: 3.7 g; Net Carbs: 6.7 g; Fiber: 1 g;

Artichoke Dip

Prep Time: 5 minutes; Cooking Time: 5 minutes; Servings: 20;

Ingredients:

- Frozen spinach – 10-ounce
- Artichoke hearts, chopped – 14 ounce
- Cloves of garlic, peeled – 3
- Onion powder – 1 teaspoon
- Mayonnaise, full-fat – ½ cup
- Parmesan cheese, grated and full-fat – 12 ounces
- Cream cheese, full-fat – 8 ounces
- Sour cream, full-fat – ½ cup
- Swiss cheese, grated, full-fat – 12 ounces

- Chicken broth, organic – ½ cup

Directions:

- Switch on an instant pot, place all the ingredients except for Swiss cheese and parmesan cheese and stir until just mixed.
- Shut instant pot with its lid, sealed completely, press manual button and cook eggs for 4 minutes at high pressure.
- When done, let the pressure release naturally for 5 minutes, then do quick pressure release and open the instant pot.
- Add Swiss and parmesan cheese into the instant pot and stir well until cheeses melt and is well combined.
- Serve immediately.

Nutritional Info:

Calories: 230.7; Fat: 18.7 g; Protein: 12.6 g; Net Carbs: 2.6 g; Fiber: 0.7 g;

Taco Meat

Prep Time: 5 minutes; Cooking Time: 8 minutes; Servings: 8;

Ingredients:

- Ground turkey – 2-pound
- Diced white onion – 1/2 cup
- Diced red bell pepper – 1/2 cup
- Tomato sauce, unsalted – 1 cup
- Taco seasoning – 1 1/2 tablespoon
- Fajita seasoning – 1 ½ tablespoon
- Avocado oil – 1 teaspoon

Directions:

- Switch on the instant pot, grease pot with oil, press the 'sauté/simmer' button, wait until the oil is hot and add the ground turkey and cook for 7 to 10 minutes or until nicely browned.
- Then add remaining ingredients, stir until mixed and press the 'keep warm' button.
- Shut the instant pot with its lid in the sealed position, then press the 'manual' button, press '+/-' to set the cooking time to 8 minutes and cook at high-pressure setting; when the pressure builds in the pot, the cooking timer will start.
- When the instant pot buzzes, press the 'keep warm' button, do a quick pressure release and open the lid.
- Transfer taco meat to a bowl, top with avocado slices, garnish with cilantro and serve.

Nutritional Info:

Calories: 231; Fat: 14 g; Protein: 21 g; Net Carbs: 2.5 g; Fiber: 1.5 g;

Green Beans with Bacon

Prep Time: 5 minutes; Cooking Time: 4 minutes; Servings: 4;

Ingredients:

- Slices of bacon, chopped – 5
- Green beans, halved – 6 cups
- Salt – 1 teaspoon
- Ground black pepper – 1 teaspoon
- Water – 1/4 cup
- Avocado oil – 2 tablespoons

Directions:

- Switch on the instant pot, place all the ingredients in it except for oil and stir until mixed.
- Shut the instant pot with its lid in the sealed position, then press the 'manual' button, press '+/-' to set the cooking time to 4 minutes and cook at high-pressure setting; when the pressure builds in the pot, the cooking timer will start.
- When the instant pot buzzes, press the 'keep warm' button, do a quick pressure release and open the lid.
- Transfer the greens and bacon to a dish, drizzle with oil, toss until well coated and serve.

Nutritional Info:

Calories: 153; Fat: 9.2 g; Protein: 7 g; Net Carbs: 4.4 g; Fiber: 5.6 g;

Beef and Broccoli

Prep Time: 5 minutes; Cooking Time: 25 minutes; Servings: 4;

Ingredients:

- Chuck roast, sliced – 1 ½ pound
- Broccoli florets – 12 ounces
- Garlic cloves, peeled – 4
- Avocado oil – 2 tablespoons
- Soy sauce – ½ cup
- Erythritol sweetener – ¼ cup
- Xanthan gum – 1 tablespoon

Directions:

- Switch on the instant pot, grease pot with oil, press the 'sauté/simmer' button, wait until the oil is hot and add the beef slices and garlic and cook for 5 to 10 minutes or until browned.
- Meanwhile, whisk together sweetener, soy sauce, and broth until combined.
- Pour sauce over browned beef, toss until well coated, then press the 'keep warm' button and shut the instant pot with its lid in the sealed position.
- Press the 'manual' button, press '+/-' to set the cooking time to 10 minutes and cook at high-pressure setting; when the pressure builds in the pot, the cooking timer will start.
- Meanwhile, place broccoli florets in a large heatproof bowl, cover with plastic wrap and microwave for 4 minutes or until tender.
- When the instant pot buzzes, press the 'keep warm' button, do a quick pressure release and open the lid.
- Take out ¼ cup of cooking liquid, stir in xanthan gum until combined, then add into the instant pot and stir until mixed.
- Press the 'sauté/simmer' button and simmer beef and sauce for 5 minutes or until the sauce reaches desired consistency.
- Then add broccoli florets, stir until mixed and press the cancel button.
- Serve broccoli and beef with cauliflower rice.

Nutritional Info:

Calories: 351.4; Fat: 12.4 g; Protein: 29 g; Net Carbs: 11 g; Fiber: 8 g;

Meatballs

Prep Time: 5 minutes; Cooking Time: 3 minutes; Yield: 35 to 40 meatballs;

Ingredients:

- Ground beef, pastured – 1 1/4 pounds
- Medium white onion, peeled, minced – 1/2
- Minced garlic – 1 tablespoon
- Ground black pepper – 1/2 teaspoon
- Salt – 1 teaspoon
- Crushed red pepper flakes – 1 teaspoon
- Fresh rosemary, chopped – 1/4 cup
- Butter, grass-fed, unsalted, softened – 2 tablespoons
- Apple cider vinegar – 1 tablespoon

Directions:

- Set oven to 350 degrees F and let preheat until meatballs are ready to bake.
- Place all the ingredients in a bowl, stir until well combined, then shape the mixture into meatballs, 1 tablespoon per meatball, and place them on a baking tray lined with parchment sheet.
- Place the baking tray into the oven and bake the meatballs for 20 minutes or until thoroughly cooked and nicely golden brown.
- When done, cool the meatballs, then place them in batches in the meal prep glass containers and refrigerate for up to 5 days or freeze for up to 3 months.
- When ready to serve, reheat the meatballs in the oven at 400 degrees F for 7 to 10 minutes or until hot.
- Serve meatballs with zucchini noodles.

Nutritional Info:

Calories: 474; Fat: 21.7 g; Protein: 61.3 g; Net Carbs: 3.1 g; Fiber: 2.5 g;

Rainbow Mason Jar Salad

Prep Time: 10 minutes; Cooking Time: 30 minutes; Yield: 1 salad jar;

Ingredients:

> For The Salad:
- Arugula, fresh – 1/2 cup
- Medium radishes, sliced – 2
- Medium yellow squash, spiralized – 1/4
- Butternut squash, peeled, cubed – 1/4 cup
- Fresh blueberries – 1/4 cup
- Avocado oil – 1 tablespoon
> The Dressing:
- Medium avocado, peeled, cubed – 1/4
- Avocado oil – 2 tablespoons
- Apple cider vinegar – 1 tablespoon
- Filtered water – 1 tablespoon
- Cilantro leaves – 1 tablespoon
- Salt – 1/4 teaspoon

Directions:

- Set oven to 350 degrees F and let preheat.
- Then place cubes of butternut squash in a bowl, drizzle with oil, toss until well coated and then spread evenly on a baking sheet.
- Place the baking sheet into the oven and bake for 30 minutes or until tender.
- Meanwhile, prepare the salad dressing and for this, place all the ingredients for the dressing in a blender and pulse for 1 to 2 minutes or until smooth, set aside until required.

- When the butternut squash is baked, take out the baking sheet from the oven and let squash cool for 15 minutes.
- Then take a 32-ounce mason jar, pour in the prepared dressing, layer with radish, and top with roasted butternut squash, squash noodles, berries, and arugula.
- Seal the jar and store in the refrigerator for up to 5 days.

Nutritional Info:

Calories: 516; Fat: 49 g; Protein: 2 g; Net Carbs: 6 g; Fiber: 6 g;

Fish Cakes

Prep Time: 10 minutes; Cooking Time: 8 minutes; Yield: 6 cakes;

Ingredients:

For Fish Cakes:
- Whitefish fillet, wild-caught – 1 pound
- Cilantro leaves and stem – 1/4 cup
- Salt – ¼ teaspoon
- Red chili flakes – 1/8 teaspoon
- Garlic cloves, peeled – 2
- Avocado oil – 2 tablespoons

Dipping Sauce:
- Avocados, peeled, pitted – 2
- Lemon, juiced – 1
- Salt – 1/8 teaspoon
- Water – 2 tablespoons

Directions:

- Prepare the fish cakes and for this, place all the ingredients for the cake in a food processor, except for oil, and pulse for 1 to 2 minutes until evenly combined.
- Then take a large skillet pan, place it on medium-high heat, add oil and leave until hot.
- Shape the fish cake mixture into six patties, then add them into the heated pan in a single layer and cook for 4 minutes per side or until thoroughly cooked and golden brown.
- When done, transfer fish patties to a plate lined with paper towels and let them rest until cooled.
- Meanwhile, prepare the sauce and for this, place all the ingredients for the dip in a blender and pulse for 1 minute until smooth and creamy.
- Place cooled fish cakes in batches in the meal prep glass containers and store in the refrigerator for up to 5 days or freeze for up to 3 months.
- When ready to serve, microwave the fish cakes in their glass container for 1 to 2 minutes or until hot.

Nutritional Info:

Calories: 69; Fat: 6.5 g; Protein: 1.1 g; Net Carbs: 0.6 g; Fiber: 2.1 g;

Lasagna Stuffed Peppers

Prep Time: 15 minutes; Cooking Time: 1 hour and 5 minutes; Yield: 6 peppers;

Ingredients:

- Large bell pepper, destemmed, cored – 6
- Ground beef, pastured – 1 1/2 pound
- Minced garlic – 2 tablespoons
- Sea salt – ¾ teaspoon

- Ground black pepper – ½ teaspoon
- Marinara sauce, organic – 2 cups
- Italian seasoning – 1 tablespoon
- Ricotta cheese, full-fat – 1 cup
- Mozzarella cheese, full-fat, shredded – 1 cup

Directions:

- Prepare the meat sauce and for this, place a skillet pan over medium-high heat, grease with oil, then add garlic and cook for 30 seconds until fragrant.
- Then add beef, stir well, cook for 10 minutes until nicely browned, season with salt, black pepper and marinara sauce, stir well and simmer the sauce for 10 minutes.
- Meanwhile, set an oven to 375 degrees F and let preheat.
- When meat sauce is cooked, remove the pan from the oven and let cool for 5 minutes.
- In the meantime, prepare the peppers and for this, cut off the tops, then scoop the inside seeds and ribs and slice slightly from the bottoms, without making any holes, so that peppers can stand upright.
- Assemble the peppers and for this, spoon 2 tablespoons of prepared meat sauce in the bottom of peppers, then evenly top with ricotta cheese and mozzarella cheese, and add two more layers in the same manner with mozzarella cheese on the top.
- Take a baking sheet, line it with aluminum foil, place the stuffed peppers on it and then tent with aluminum foil.
- Place the baking sheet into the oven, bake for 30 minutes, then remove the aluminum foil and continue baking for 10 minutes or until cheese melts and slightly browned.
- Cool the stuffed pepper at room temperature, then wrap each pepper with aluminum foil and store in the freezer for about 2 to 3 minutes.
- When ready to serve, reheat the peppers into the oven at 350 degrees F for 5 minutes or until hot.

Nutritional Info:

Calories: 412; Fat: 27 g; Protein: 30 g; Net Carbs: 8 g; Fiber: 2 g;

Korean Ground Beef Bowl

Prep Time: 10 minutes; Cooking Time: 20 minutes; Yield: 4 bowls;

Ingredients:

    For Cauliflower Rice:
- Cauliflower, riced – 1 pound
- Sea salt – 1/2 teaspoon
- Ground black pepper – 1/8 teaspoon
- Avocado oil – 1 tablespoon
  For the Beef:
- Beef, grass-fed – 1 pound
- Sea salt – 1/2 teaspoon
- Minced garlic – 2 tablespoons
- Coconut aminos – 1/4 cup
- Ground ginger – 1/4 teaspoon
- Crushed red pepper flakes – 1/4 teaspoon
- Avocado oil – 1 tablespoon
- Sesame oil – 2 teaspoons
- Beef broth, grass-fed – 1/4 cup
  For the Garnish:
- Sliced Green onions – 1/4 cup
- Sesame seeds – 1 teaspoon

Directions:

- Prepare cauliflower rice and for this, take a large skillet pan, place it over medium-high heat, add oil and when hot, add

- cauliflower rice, season with salt and black pepper and cook for 5 minutes or until thoroughly cooked.
- Then remove the pan from the heat, transfer to a bowl, and set aside until required.
- Prepare the sauce and for this, whisk together ginger, coconut aminos, red pepper flakes, sesame oil, and beef broth until combined, and set aside until required.
- Return skillet pan over medium-high heat, add avocado oil and when hot, add beef, season with salt and cook for 10 minutes or until light brown.
- Make the well in the pan, add garlic in it, and let it cook for 1 minute or until sauté, then mix it into the beef and pour in the prepared sauce.
- Stir well and let beef simmer for 4 minutes or until sauce is thickened and not much liquid is left in the pan.
- Remove pan from the heat and let beef cool completely.
- Portion out the beef and cauliflower into four glass meal prep containers, garnish with green onion and sesame seeds, then cover with lid and store in the refrigerator for up to 5 days or freeze for up to 2 months.
- When ready to serve, reheat the beef and cauliflower in its glass container in the microwave for 1 to 2 minutes or until hot.

Nutritional Info: Calories: 513; Fat: 36 g; Protein: 35 g; Net Carbs: 9 g; Fiber: 3 g;

Snack and Sides

Asparagus Fries

Prep Time: 10 minutes; Cooking Time: 10 minutes; Servings: 2;

Ingredients:

- Medium organic asparagus spears – 10
- Organic roasted red pepper, chopped – 1 tablespoon
- Almond flour – ¼ cup
- Garlic powder – ½ teaspoon
- Smoked paprika – ½ teaspoon
- Chopped parsley – 2 tablespoons
- Parmesan cheese, grated and full-fat – ½ cup
- Organic eggs, beaten – 2
- Mayonnaise, full-fat – 3 tablespoon

Directions:

- Set oven to 425 degrees F and preheat.
- Meanwhile, place cheese in a food processor, add garlic and parsley and pulse for 1 minute until fine mixture comes together.
- Add almond flour, pulse for 30 seconds until just mixed, then tip the mixture into a bowl and season with paprika.
- Crack eggs into a shallow dish and whisk until beaten.
- Working on one asparagus spear at a time, first dip into the egg mixture, then coat with parmesan mixture and place it on a baking sheet.
- Dip and coat more asparagus in the same manner, then arrange them on a baking sheet, 1-inch apart, and bake in the oven for 10 minutes or until asparagus is tender and nicely golden brown.

- Meanwhile, place mayonnaise in a bowl, add red pepper and whisk until combined and chill the dip into the refrigerator until required.
- Serve asparagus with prepared dip.

Nutritional Info:

Calories: 453; Fat: 33.4 g; Protein: 19.1 g; Net Carbs: 5.5 g; Fiber: 3.75 g;

Kale Chips

Prep Time: 5 minutes; Cooking Time: 12 minutes; Servings: 4;

Ingredients:

- Large bunch of organic kale – 1
- Seasoned salt – 1 tablespoon
- Olive oil – 2 tablespoons

Directions:

- Set oven to 350 degrees F and preheat.
- Meanwhile, separate kale leaves from its stem, rinse the leaves under running water, then drain completely by using a vegetable spinner.
- Wipe kale leaves with paper towels to remove excess water, then transfer them into a large plastic bag and add oil.
- Seal the plastic bag, turn it upside down until kale is coated with oil and then spread kale leaves on a large baking sheet.
- Place the baking sheet into the oven and bake for 12 minutes or until its edges are nicely golden brown.

- Remove baking sheet from the oven, season kale with salt and serve.

Nutritional Info:

Calories: 163; Fat: 10 g; Protein: 2 g; Net Carbs: 14 g; Fiber: 2 g;

Guacamole

Prep Time: 10 minutes; Cooking Time: 0 minutes; Servings: 4;

Ingredients:

- Organic avocados, pitted – 2
- Medium organic red onion, peeled and sliced – 1/3
- Medium organic jalapeño, deseeded and diced – 1
- Salt – ½ teaspoon
- Ground pepper – ½ teaspoon
- Tomato salsa, organic – 2 tablespoons
- Lime juice, organic – 1 tablespoon
- Bunch of organic cilantro – ½

Directions:

- Cut each avocado into half, remove its pit and slice its flesh horizontally and vertically.
- Scoop out the flesh of the avocado, place it in a bowl and add onion, jalapeno, and lime juice then stir until well mixed.
- Season with salt and black pepper, add salsa and stir with a fork until avocado is mash to desired consistency.
- Fold in cilantro and serve.

Nutritional Info:

Calories: 16.5; Fat: 1.4 g; Protein: 0.23 g; Net Carbs: 0.5 g; Fiber: 0.6 g;

Zucchini Noodles

Prep Time: 5 minutes; Cooking Time: 6 minutes; Servings: 2;
Ingredients:
- Medium zucchini, spiralized into noodles – 2
- Butter, unsalted – 2 tablespoons
- Minced garlic – 1 ½ tablespoon
- Parmesan cheese, grated – 3/4 cup
- Sea salt – ½ teaspoon
- Ground black pepper – ¼ teaspoon
- Red chili flakes – ¼ teaspoon

Directions:
- Switch on the instant pot, add butter, press the 'sauté/simmer' button, wait until the butter melts, and add garlic and cook for 1 minute or until fragrant.
- Add zucchini noodles, toss until coated, cook for 5 minutes or until tender and season with salt and black pepper.
- Press the 'keep warm' button, then transfer to noodles to a dish, top with cheese and sprinkle with red chili flakes.
- Serve straight away.

Nutritional Info:
Calories: 298; Fat: 26.1 g; Protein: 5 g; Net Carbs: 2.3 g; Fiber: 0.1 g;

Cauliflower Souffle

Prep Time: 10 minutes; Cooking Time: 12 minutes; Servings: 6;

Ingredients:

- Large head of Cauliflower, cut into small florets – 1
- Eggs – 2
- Heavy Cream – 2 tablespoons
- Cream Cheese – 2 ounces
- Sour Cream – 1/2 cup
- Asiago cheese – 1/2 cup
- Sharp Cheddar Cheese, grated – 1 cup
- Chives – ¼ cup
- Butter, unsalted – 2 tablespoons
- slices of bacon, sugar-free, cooked, crumbled – 6
- Water – 1 cup

Directions:

- Crack eggs in a food processor, add heavy cream, sour cream, cream cheese, and cheeses and pulse until smooth.
- Add cauliflower florets, pulse for 2 seconds or until folded and chunky, then add butter and chives and pulse for another 2 seconds.
- Switch on the instant pot, pour in water, and insert a trivet stand.
- Pour the cauliflower mixture in a greased round casserole dish that fits into the instant pot, smooth the top and place the dish on the trivet stand.
- Shut the instant pot with its lid in the sealed position, then press the 'manual' button, press '+/-' to set the cooking time to 12 minutes and cook at high-pressure setting; when the pressure builds in the pot, the cooking timer will start.

- When the instant pot buzzes, press the 'keep warm' button, release pressure naturally for 10 minutes, then do a quick pressure release and open the lid.
- Take out the casserole dish, top with bacon, and serve.

Nutritional Info:

Calories: 342; Fat: 28 g; Protein: 17 g; Net Carbs: 5 g; Fiber: 2 g;

Carnitas

Prep Time: 5 minutes; Cooking Time: 55 minutes; Servings: 8;

Ingredients:

- Pork shoulder, fat trimmed, 2-inch sliced – 3 pounds
- Garlic powder – 2 teaspoons
- Cumin – 2 teaspoons
- Coriander – 1 teaspoon
- Sea salt – 1 teaspoon
- Avocado oil – 3 tablespoons
- Salsa Verde – 12 ounces
- Lime juice – 1/2 cup

Directions:

- Stir together garlic, cumin, coriander, and salt until mixed, and then sprinkle on both sides of the pork until evenly coated.
- Switch on the instant pot, grease pot with oil, press the 'sauté/simmer' button, wait until the oil is hot and add the pork pieces in a single layer and cook for 5 minutes per side or until browned.

- Return all the browned pork slices in the instant pot, top with salsa and lime juice, press the 'keep warm' button and shut the instant pot with its lid in the sealed position.
- Press the 'meat/stew' button, press '+/-' to set the cooking time to 35 minutes and cook at high-pressure setting; when the pressure builds in the pot, the cooking timer will start.
- When the instant pot buzzes, press the 'keep warm' button, do a quick pressure release and open the lid.
- Press the 'sauté/simmer' button and cook until cooking liquid is reduced by half or more.
- Serve straight away.

Nutritional Info:

Calories: 242; Fat: 15 g; Protein: 20 g; Net Carbs: 3.5 g; Fiber: 2.5 g;

Brussels Sprouts

Prep Time: 5 minutes; Cooking Time: 9 minutes; Servings: 4;

Ingredients:

- Avocado oil – 2 tablespoons
- White onion, peeled, chopped – 1/2 cup
- Minced garlic – 2 teaspoons
- Strips of bacon, chopped – 3
- Brussels sprouts, outer leaves trimmed – 1 pound
- Water – 1/2 cup
- Salt – 1 teaspoon
- Ground black pepper – ½ teaspoon
- Parmesan cheese, grated – ¼ cup

Directions:

- Switch on the instant pot, grease pot with oil, press the 'sauté/simmer' button, wait until the oil is hot and add the onion garlic and cook for 1 minute or more until sautéd.
- Then add bacon, continue cooking for 5 minutes or until bacon is crispy, add sprouts, season with salt and black pepper and pour in water.
- Press the 'keep warm' button, shut the instant pot with its lid in the sealed position, then press the 'manual' button, press '+/-' to set the cooking time to 3 minutes and cook at low pressure setting; when the pressure builds in the pot, the cooking timer will start.
- When the instant pot buzzes, press the 'keep warm' button, do a quick pressure release and open the lid.
- Drain the liquid, transfer the sprouts to a dish, drizzle with more oil, sprinkle with parmesan cheese, toss until well mixed and serve.

Nutritional Info:

Calories: 312; Fat: 20 g; Protein: 13 g; Net Carbs: 4 g; Fiber: 4 g;

Cauliflower Mashed Potatoes

Prep Time: 5 minutes; Cooking Time: 6 minutes; Servings: 4;

Ingredients:

- Large head of cauliflower, cut into florets – 1
- Avocado oil – 1 tablespoon
- Sour cream – 1/3 cup
- Butter, salted – 3 tablespoons
- Cloves of garlic, peeled, sliced – 2
- Parmesan cheese, grated – ¼ cup
- Salt – 1 teaspoon

- Ground black pepper – 1 teaspoon
- Water – 1 cup

Directions:

- Switch on the instant pot, pour water in it, insert a steel steamer rack and place florets on it.
- Shut the instant pot with its lid in the sealed position, then press the 'manual' button, press '+/-' to set the cooking time to 5 minutes and cook at high-pressure setting; when the pressure builds in the pot, the cooking timer will start.
- When the instant pot buzzes, press the 'keep warm' button, do a quick pressure release and open the lid.
- Transfer florets into a blender, add oil, salt, black pepper, and sour cream and pulse until blended.
- Drain the instant pot, press the 'sauté/simmer' button, wait until it gets hot, then add butter and when it melts, add garlic and cook for 1 minute or until browned and fragrant.
- Ladle the butter-garlic mixture into the food processor, add cheese and blend again until smooth.
- Tip the mixture into a dish, garnish with thyme and serve.

Nutritional Info:

Calories: 198; Fat: 17 g; Protein: 5 g; Net Carbs: 4 g; Fiber: 3 g;

Teriyaki Drumsticks

Prep Time: 5 minutes; Cooking Time: 15 minutes; Servings: 4;

Ingredients:

- Soy sauce – 1/4 cup

- Apple cider vinegar – 2 tablespoons
- Stevia, liquid – 2 tablespoons
- Minced garlic – 1 teaspoon
- Grated ginger – 1 teaspoon
- Sriracha sauce – 1 teaspoon
- Sesame oil – 1 tablespoon
- Drumsticks, skinless – 28 oz
- Sesame seeds – 1 tablespoon

Directions:

- Switch on the instant pot, grease pot with oil, press the 'sauté/simmer' button, wait until the oil is hot and add all the ingredients except for the drumsticks and sesame seeds, stir well and cook for 2 minutes.
- Add chicken drumsticks, toss until well coated, then press the 'keep warm' button and shut the instant pot with its lid in the sealed position.
- Press the 'manual' button, press '+/-' to set the cooking time to 15 minutes and cook at high-pressure setting; when the pressure builds in the pot, the cooking timer will start.
- When the instant pot buzzes, press the 'keep warm' button, release pressure naturally for 10 minutes, then do a quick pressure release and open the lid.
- Transfer chicken drumsticks to a dish, garnish with sesame seeds and serve.

Nutritional Info:

Calories: 192; Fat: 13 g; Protein: 17 g; Net Carbs: 1 g; Fiber: 0 g;

Cheesy Garlic Spaghetti Squash

Prep Time: 10 minutes; Cooking Time: 20 minutes; Servings: 4;

Ingredients:

- Spaghetti squash – 2 pounds
- Water – 1 cup
- Butter, unsalted – 4 tablespoons
- Minced garlic – 2 tablespoons
- Broccoli florets, cut into bite-sized pieces – 1 cup
- Chicken broth – 2 tablespoons
- Parmesan cheese, grated – 1/2 cup
- Mozzarella cheese, shredded – ½ cup
- Ground black pepper – 1 teaspoon
- Avocado oil – 2 tablespoons

Directions:

- Switch on the instant pot, pour in water, and insert a steel steamer rack.
- Make one inch cuts into the skin of the squash, about 1-inch apart and place them on the trivet stand.
- Shut the instant pot with its lid in the sealed position, then press the 'manual' button, press '+/-' to set the cooking time to 15 minutes and cook at high-pressure setting; when the pressure builds in the pot, the cooking timer will start.
- When the instant pot buzzes, press the 'keep warm' button, do a quick pressure release and open the lid.
- Take out the spaghetti squash and let it cool for 10 minutes.
- Then drain the instant pot, press the 'sauté/simmer' button, wait until it is hot, then add butter and garlic and cook for 2 minutes or until butter melts, and garlic is browned.
- Add broccoli florets, drizzle with broth, cook for 3 minutes or until tender-crisp and then press the 'keep warm' button.
- Cut squash in half, lengthwise, remove its seeds, then shred its meat with a fork and add into the instant pot.

- Add cheeses in the squash, toss until squash is evenly coated with cheese and cheese melts completely.
- Garnish squash with black pepper, drizzle with oil and serve with tomato curry or meatballs.

Nutritional Info:

Calories: 254; Fat: 24 g; Protein: 10 g; Net Carbs: 7 g; Fiber: 5 g;

Dinner

Sriracha Tuna Kabobs

Prep time: 4 minutes
Cook time: 9 minutes
Number of Servings: 4

Ingredients
- 4 tablespoon Huy Fong chili garlic sauce
- 1 tablespoon sesame oil infused with garlic
- 1 tablespoon ginger, fresh, grated
- 1 tablespoon garlic, minced
- 1 red onion, cut into quarters and separated by petals
- 2 cups bell peppers, red, green, yellow
- 1 can whole water chestnuts, cut in half
- ½ pound fresh mushrooms halved
- 32 oz. boneless tuna, chunks or steaks
- 1 Splenda packet
- 2 zucchini, sliced
- 1 inch thick, keep skins on

Directions
1. Layer the tuna and the vegetable pieces evenly onto 8 skewers.
2. Combine the spices and the oil and chili sauce, add the Splenda
3. Quickly blend, either in a blender or by Quickly whipping.
4. Brush onto the kabob pieces, make sure every piece is coated
5. Grill 4 minutes on each side, check to ensure the tuna is cooked to taste.

6. Serving size is two skewers.
7. Mix the marinade ingredients and store in a covered container in the fridge. Place all the vegetables in one container in the fridge.
8. Place the tuna in a separate zip-lock bag.

Nutritional Value:
Calories: 467,
Total Fat: 18g,
Protein: 56g,
Total Carbs: 21g,
Dietary Fiber: 3.5g,
Sugar: 6g,
Sodium: 433mg

Chicken Relleno Casserole

Prep time: 19 minutes

Cook time: 29 minutes

Number of Servings: 4

Ingredients

- 6 Tortilla Factory low-carb whole wheat tortillas, torn into small pieces
- 1 ½ cups hand-shredded cheese, Mexican
- 1 beaten egg
- 1 cup milk
- 2 cups cooked chicken, shredded

- 1 can Ro-tel
- ½ cup salsa verde

Directions

1. Grease an 8 x 8 glass baking dish
2. Heat oven to 375 degrees
3. Combine everything, but reserve ½ cup of the cheese
4. Bake it for 29 minutes
5. Take it out of the oven and add ½ cup cheese
6. Broil for about 2 minutes to melt the cheese
7. Let the casserole cool. Slice into 6 pieces and place in freezer containers, (1 cup with a lid) Freeze. Microwave for 2 minutes to serve. Top with sour cream, if desired.

Nutritional Value:

Calories: 265,

Total Fat: 16g,

Protein: 20g,

Total Carbs: 18g,

Dietary Fiber: 10g,

Sugar: 0g,

Sodium: 708mg

Steak Salad with Asian Spice

Prep time: 4 minutes
Cook time: 4 minutes
Number of Servings: 2

Ingredients

- 2 tablespoon sriracha sauce
- 1 tablespoon garlic, minced
- 1 tablespoon ginger, fresh, grated
- 1 bell pepper, yellow, cut into thin strips
- 1 bell pepper, red, cut into thin strips
- 1 tablespoon sesame oil, garlic
- 1 Splenda packet
- ½ tablespoon curry powder
- ½ tablespoon rice wine vinegar
- 8 oz. of beef sirloin, cut into strips
- 2 cups baby spinach, stemmed
- ½ head butter lettuce, torn or chopped into bite-sized pieces

Directions

1. Place the garlic, sriracha sauce, 1 tablespoon sesame oil, rice wine vinegar, and Splenda into a bowl and combine well.
2. Pour half of this mix into a zip-lock bag. Add the steak to marinade while you are preparing the salad.
3. Assemble the brightly colored salad by layering in two bowls.
4. Place the baby spinach into the bottom of the bowl. Place the butter lettuce next.
5. Mix the two peppers and place on top.
6. Remove the steak from the marinade and discard the liquid and bag.
7. Heat the sesame oil and quickly stir fry the steak until desired doneness, it should take about 3 minutes.
8. Place the steak on top of the salad.

9. Drizzle with the remaining dressing (another half of marinade mix).
10. Sprinkle sriracha sauce across the salad.
11. Combine the salad ingredients and place in a zip-lock bag in the fridge. Mix the marinade and halve into 2 zip-lock bags. Place the sriracha sauce into a small sealed container. Slice the steak and freeze in a zip-lock bag with the marinade. To prepare, mix the ingredients like the initial directions. Stir fry the marinated beef for 4 minutes to take into consideration the beef is frozen.

Nutritional Value:
Calories: 350; Total Fat: 23g; Protein: 28g; Total Carbs: 7g; Dietary Fiber: 3.5; Sugar: 0; Sodium: 267mg.

Chicken Chow Mein Stir Fry

Prep time: 9 minutes
Cook time: 14 minutes
Number of Servings: 4

Ingredients
- 1/2 cup sliced onion
- 2 tablespoon Oil, sesame garlic flavored
- 4 cups shredded Bok-Choy
- 1 cup Sugar Snap Peas
- 1 cup fresh bean sprouts
- 3 stalks Celery, chopped
- 1 1/2 tablespoon minced Garlic
- 1 packet Splenda
- 1 cup Broth, chicken

- 2 tablespoon Soy Sauce
- 1 tablespoon ginger, freshly minced
- 1 tablespoon cornstarch
- 4 boneless Chicken Breasts, cooked/sliced thinly

Directions
1. Place the bok-choy, peas, celery in a skillet with 1 T garlic oil.
2. Stir fry until bok-choy is softened to liking.
3. Add remaining ingredients except for the cornstarch.
4. If too thin, stir cornstarch into ½ cup cold water when smooth pour into skillet.
5. Bring cornstarch and chow mein to a one-minute boil. Turn off the heat source.
6. Stir sauce then wait for 4 minutes to serve, after the chow mein has thickened.
7. Freeze in covered containers. Heat for 2 minutes in the microwave before serving.

Nutritional Value:
Calories: 368, Total Fat: 18g, Protein: 42g, Total Carbs: 12g, Dietary Fiber: 16g, Sugar: 6g, Sodium: 746mg.

Salmon with Bok-Choy

Prep time: 9 minutes
Cook time: 9 minutes
Number of Servings: 4

Ingredients
- 1 cup red peppers, roasted, drained
- 2 cups chopped bok-choy

- 1 tablespoon salted butter
- 5 oz. salmon steak
- 1 lemon, sliced very thinly
- 1/8 tablespoon black pepper
- 1 tablespoon olive oil
- 2 tablespoon sriracha sauce

Directions
1. Place oil in a skillet
2. Place all but 4 slices of lemon in the skillet.
3. Sprinkle the bok choy with the black pepper.
4. Stir fry the bok-choy with the lemons.
5. Remove and place on four plates.
6. Place the butter in the skillet and stir fry the salmon, turning once.
7. Place the salmon on the bed of bok-choy.
8. Divide the red peppers and encircle the salmon.
9. Place a slice of lemon atop the salmon.
10. Drizzle with sriracha sauce.
11. Freeze the cooked salmon in individual zip-lock bags. Place the bok-choy, with the remaining ingredients into one-cup containers. Microwave the salmon for one minute and the frozen bok choy for two. Assemble to serve.

Nutritional Value:
Calories: 410, Total Fat: 30g, Protein: 30g, Total Carbs: 7g, Dietary Fiber: 2g, Sugar: 0g, Sodium: 200mg.

Whole Chicken

Prep Time: 5 minutes; Cooking Time: 25 minutes; Servings: 7;

Ingredients:

- Medium whole chicken – 5 pounds
- Minced garlic – 1 ½ teaspoon
- Avocado oil – 1 tablespoon
- Sea salt – 1/8 teaspoon
- Ground black pepper – ¼ teaspoon
- Lemon, sliced – 1
- Water – 2 cups
- Apple cider vinegar – 1 tablespoon

Directions:

- Brush chicken with oil, then rub with salt and black pepper and stuff its cavity with lemon slices.
- Switch on the instant pot, pour in water, add vinegar, then place the chicken on it and shut the instant pot with its lid in the sealed position.
- Press the 'manual' button, press '+/-' to set the cooking time to 25 minutes and cook at high-pressure setting; when the pressure builds in the pot, the cooking timer will start.
- When the instant pot buzzes, press the 'keep warm' button, release pressure naturally for 10 minutes, then do a quick pressure release and open the lid.
- Transfer chicken to a cutting board, let it rest for 10 minutes, then cut into pieces and serve.

Nutritional Info:

Calories: 209; Fat: 5 g; Protein: 41 g; Net Carbs: 1 g; Fiber: 0 g;

Lamb Shanks

Prep Time: 5 minutes; Cooking Time: 1 hour and 30 minutes; Servings: 2;

Ingredients:

- Avocado oil – 1/4 cup
- Lamb shanks – 2.5 pounds
- Minced garlic – 1 tablespoon
- Medium white onion, peeled and diced – 1
- Sticks of celery, diced – 2
- Rosemary – 2 tablespoons
- Salt – 1 teaspoon
- Ground black pepper – 1/2 teaspoon
- Lamb or chicken broth – 1 cup
- Diced tomatoes – 14 ounces

Directions:

- Switch on the instant pot, add half of the oil, press the 'sauté/simmer' button, wait until the oil is hot and lamb shanks in a single layer and cook for 3 to 5 minutes per side or until browned.
- Transfer lamb shanks to a plate, set aside, then add onion, celery, garlic, and rosemary into the instant pot and cook for 3 minutes.
- Season with salt and black pepper, pour in the broth, mix well, then add tomatoes, return lamb shanks into the pot and toss until combined.
- Press the 'keep warm' button, shut the instant pot with its lid in the sealed position, then press the 'manual' button, press '+/-' to set the cooking time to 50 minutes and cook at high-pressure setting; when the pressure builds in the pot, the cooking timer will start.
- When the instant pot buzzes, press the 'keep warm' button, release pressure naturally for 10 minutes, then do a quick pressure release and open the lid.

- Transfer lamb shanks to a dish, then press the 'sauté/simmer' button and simmer the sauce for 5 minutes or more until the sauce is reduced by half.
- Ladle sauce over the lamb shanks and serve.

Nutritional Info:

Calories: 410; Fat: 35 g; Protein: 51 g; Net Carbs: 12 g; Fiber: 3 g;

Jamaican Jerk Pork Roast

Prep Time: 5 minutes; Cooking Time: 1 hour and 5 minutes; Servings: 4;

Ingredients:

- Pork shoulder, fat trimmed – 4 pounds
- Jamaican jerk spice mix – 1/4 cup
- Avocado oil – 2 tablespoons
- Beef broth – 1/2 cup

Directions:

- Brush pork shoulder with 1 tablespoon oil and then sprinkle with spice mix until evenly coated on all sides.
- Switch on the instant pot, grease pot with oil, press the 'sauté/simmer' button, wait until the oil is hot, add pork shoulder and cook for 5 minutes per side or until nicely browned.
- Pour in beef broth,
- Press the 'keep warm' button, shut the instant pot with its lid in the sealed position, then press the 'manual' button, press '+/-' to set the cooking time to 45 minutes and cook at high-

pressure setting; when the pressure builds in the pot, the cooking timer will start.
- When the instant pot buzzes, press the 'keep warm' button, release pressure naturally for 10 minutes, then do a quick pressure release and open the lid.
- Shred the pork with two forks, toss until mixed and serve.

Nutritional Info:

Calories: 282; Fat: 20 g; Protein: 23 g; Net Carbs: 0 g; Fiber: 0 g;

Mexican Shredded Beef

Prep Time: 10 minutes; Cooking Time: 7 hours and 15 minutes; Yield: 8;

Ingredients:

- Beef short ribs, grass-fed – 3 1/2 pounds
- Minced garlic – 2 tablespoons
- Ground turmeric – 2 teaspoons
- Salt – 1 teaspoon
- Ground black pepper – 1/2 teaspoon
- Ground cumin – 2 teaspoons
- Ground coriander – 2 teaspoons
- Chipotle powder – 1 teaspoon
- Water – 1/2 cup
- Cilantro stems, chopped – 1 cup

Directions:

- Place salt in a small bowl, add black pepper, cumin, coriander, chipotle powder and stir until mixed.

- Place ribs into the slow cooker, sprinkle well with the prepared spice mix and then top with minced garlic and cilantro stems.
- Switch on the slow cooker, pour in water, then cover with the lid and cook for 6 to 7 hours over low heat setting or until tender.
- Then pour the sauce into a small saucepan and cook for 10 to 15 minutes or until reduced by half.
- Return the sauce into the slow cooker, pull apart the meat and toss until well mixed.
- Portion out beef into eight glass meal prep containers, then cover with lid and store in the refrigerator for up to 5 days or freeze for up to 2 months.
- When ready to serve, reheat the beef in its glass container in the microwave for 1 to 2 minutes or until hot.

Nutritional Info:

Calories: 656; Fat: 48.5 g; Protein: 50.2 g; Net Carbs: 1 g; Fiber: 0.4 g;

Beef Stew

Prep Time: 5 minutes; Cooking Time: 8 hours and 5 minutes; Yield: 4;

Ingredients:

- Beef, grass-fed, diced – 3 1/2 pounds
- Stalks of celery, chopped – 3
- Leek, white part only – 1
- Diced tomatoes – 15 ounces
- Spinach leaves, fresh – ¾ cup
- Carrots, chopped into large rounds – 3

- Chopped ginger – 1 tablespoon
- Minced garlic – ½ tablespoon
- Salt – 1 ½ teaspoon
- Ground black pepper – ¾ teaspoon
- Dried rosemary – 2 teaspoons
- Dried thyme – 2 teaspoons
- Dried oregano – 2 teaspoons
- Apple cider vinegar – 2 tablespoons
- Avocado oil – 2 tablespoons
- Beef broth, grass-fed – 1 1/2 cups

Directions:

- Take a frying pan, place it over medium heat, add oil and when hot, add beef and cook for 3 to 5 minutes or until light brown.
- Transfer beef into a slow cooker, add remaining ingredients, except for spinach and stir until mixed.
- Switch on the slow cooker, shut it with lid and cook for 5 to 8 hours at low heat setting until thoroughly cooked.
- When beef cooking is about to finish, place spinach in a heatproof bowl, cover with plastic wrap and microwave for 2 minutes until steamed.
- When beef is cooked, taste to adjust seasoning, add spinach, and stir until just mixed and let cool.
- Divide beef evenly between four glass containers, then cover with lid and store in the refrigerator for up to 5 days or freeze for up to 2 months.
- When ready to serve, thaw the stew at room temperature and then reheat the beef stew in its glass container in the microwave for 2 to 3 minutes or until hot.
- Serve the stew with cauliflower rice.

Nutritional Info:

Calories: 553; Fat: 36.9 g; Protein: 175 g; Net Carbs: 4.8 g; Fiber: 1.6 g;

Coconut Shrimp

Prep Time: 10 minutes; Cooking Time: 12 minutes; Yield: 4;

Ingredients:

- Medium-sized shrimp, wild-caught, peeled, deveined – 1 pound
- Coconut flour – 3 tablespoons
- Garlic powder – 1/4 teaspoon
- Eggs, Pastured, beaten – 3
- Coconut flakes, unsweetened – 1 3/4 cup
- Ground black pepper – 1/8 teaspoon
- Smoked paprika – 1/4 teaspoon
- Sea salt – 1/4 teaspoon

Directions:

- Set the oven to 400 degrees F and let preheat.
- Meanwhile, crack eggs in a bowl and whisk until beaten, place coconut flakes in another dish, then place coconut flour in another dish, add salt, black pepper, garlic powder, and paprika and stir until mixed.
- Working on one piece at a time, dredge a shrimp into the coconut flour mix, then dip into egg, and dredge with coconut flake until evenly coated.
- Take a non-stick wire rack, line it with a baking sheet, then spray with oil and place coated shrimps on it in a single layer.

- Place the wire rack containing shrimps into the oven, bake for 4 minutes, then flip the shrimps and continue baking for 5 to 6 minutes or until thoroughly cooked and firm.
- Then switch on the broiler and bake the shrimps for 2 minutes or until lightly golden.
- When done, let shrimps cooled, place them on a baking sheet in a single layer, then cover the shrimps with parchment sheet, layer with remaining shrimps and freeze until hard.
- Then transfer shrimps into a freezer bag and store in the freezer for up to 3 months.
- When ready to serve, reheat the shrimps at 350 degrees F for 2 to 3 minutes until hot.

Nutritional Info:

Calories: 443; Fat: 30 g; Protein: 31 g; Net Carbs: 5 g; Fiber: 7 g;

Sausage Stuffed Zucchini Boats

Prep Time: 10 minutes; Cooking Time: 30 minutes; Yield: 4;

Ingredients:

- Medium zucchini – 4
- Ground Italian pork sausage, pastured – 1 pound
- Sea salt – 1 ½ teaspoon
- Medium white onion, peeled, diced – 1/3 cup
- Minced garlic – 1 tablespoon
- Italian seasoning – 1 teaspoon
- Diced tomatoes – 14.5 ounces
- Grated parmesan cheese, full-fat – 1/3 cup
- Avocado oil, divided – 2 tablespoons
- Mozzarella cheese, full-fat, shredded – 1 cup

Directions:

- Set oven to 400 degrees F and let preheat.
- Meanwhile, cut each zucchini in half, lengthwise, then make well in the center by scooping out the centers by using a spoon.
- Take a baking sheet, line it with parchment sheet, place zucchini halves on it, cut side up, drizzle with 1 tablespoon oil and season with salt.
- Place the baking sheet into the oven and bake for 15 to 20 minutes or until soft.
- Meanwhile, take a large skillet pan, place it over medium-high heat, add remaining oil and when hot, add onions and cook for 10 minutes until nicely brown.
- Add sausage, stir well and cook for 5 minutes or until brown.
- Then move sausage to one side of the pan, add garlic to the other side, cook for 1 minute or until fragrant and then mix into the sausage.
- Remove pan from the heat, season sausage with Italian seasoning, add tomatoes and parmesan cheese, stir well and taste to adjust seasoning.
- When zucchini halves are roasted, pat dry with paper towels, then stuff with sausage mixture.
- Top stuffed zucchini with mozzarella cheese and bake for 5 to 10 minutes or until cheese melts, and the top is nicely golden brown.
- Let zucchini boats cool down, then wrap each zucchini boat with an aluminum foil and freeze in the freezer.
- When ready to serve, thaw the zucchini boat and reheat at 350 degrees F for 3 to 4 minutes until hot.

Nutritional Info:

Calories: 582; Fat: 44 g; Protein: 29 g; Net Carbs: 11 g; Fiber: 3 g;

Balsamic Steaks

Prep Time: 3 hours and 10 minutes; Cooking Time: 10 minutes; Yield: 4;

Ingredients:

- Sirloin steaks, grass-fed – 4, each about 8 ounces
- Butter, grass-fed, unsalted – 1 tablespoon
  For the marinade:
- Garlic powder – 1/2 teaspoon
- Coconut aminos – 1/4 cup
- Ground black pepper – 1/2 teaspoon
- Avocado oil – 1/4 cup
- Balsamic vinegar – 2 tablespoons
- Italian seasoning – 1 teaspoon
- Sea salt – 1 teaspoon

Directions:

- Place all the ingredients for the marinade in a bowl, whisk until well combined and then pour the mixture in a large freezer bag.
- Add steaks into the bag, seal the bag, then turn it upside side or until steaks are coated with the marinade and place it in the refrigerator for 3 hours.
- When ready to cook, set the oven to 400 degrees F and let preheat.
- In the meantime, take out steaks from the refrigerator and let rest at the room temperature.
- Then take a large skillet pan, place it over medium heat, add butter and when it melts, add steaks in a single layer and cook for 2 minutes per side or until seared.

- Transfer the pan into the oven and bake the steaks for 3 to 6 minutes or until cooked to desired doneness, such as 3 minutes or 120 degrees F for medium-rare doneness, 4 minutes or 140 degrees F for medium doneness, 5 minutes or 150 degrees F for medium-well doneness and 6 minutes or 160 degrees F for well-done steak.
- Transfer the steaks to a plate, let them rest for 5 minutes and cut into slices.
- Then transfer steaks into a freezer bag and store in the freezer for up to 3 months.
- When ready to serve, reheat the steak slices into a hot skillet pan until warm through.

Nutritional Info:

Calories: 450; Fat: 24 g; Protein: 49 g; Net Carbs: 5 g; Fiber: 0 g;

Salmon

Prep Time: 5 minutes; Cooking Time: 5 minutes; Servings: 4;

Ingredients:

- Lemon, sliced – 3
- Water – 3/4 cup
- Salmon fillets – 4
- Bunch of dill weed, fresh – 1
- Butter, unsalted – 1 tablespoon
- Salt – 1/4 teaspoon
- Ground black pepper – 1/4 teaspoon

Directions:

- Switch on the instant pot, pour in water, stir in lemon juice, and insert a steel steamer rack.
- Place salmon on the steamer rack, sprinkle with dill and then top with lemon slices.
- Press the 'keep warm' button, shut the instant pot with its lid in the sealed position, then press the 'manual' button, press '+/-' to set the cooking time to 5 minutes and cook at high-pressure setting; when the pressure builds in the pot, the cooking timer will start.
- When the instant pot buzzes, press the 'keep warm' button, do a quick pressure release and open the lid.
- Remove and discard the lemon slices, transfer salmon to a dish, season with salt and black pepper, garnish with more dill and serve with lemon wedges and cauliflower rice.

Nutritional Info:

Calories: 199.2; Fat: 8.1 g; Protein: 29.2 g; Net Carbs: 0.8 g; Fiber: 0.1 g;

Sweet and Spicy Barbecue Chicken Wings

Prep Time: 10 minutes; Cooking Time: 35 minutes; Servings: 6;

Ingredients:

- Chicken wings – 2 pounds
- Salt – 1 tablespoon
  For Barbecue Sauce:
- Liquid smoke – 1 teaspoon
- Tomato paste – 4 ounces
- Red hot sauce – 1/4 cup
- Apple cider vinegar – 1/2 cup

- Water – 1/2 cup
- Cayenne pepper – 1/8 teaspoon
- Ground chipotle pepper – 1/8 teaspoon
- Crushed red pepper flakes – 1/4 teaspoon
- Paprika – 1/2 teaspoon
- Cinnamon – 1 teaspoon
- Salt – 1 teaspoon
- Erythritol sweetener – 2 1/2 tablespoons

Directions:

- Prepare BBQ sauce and for this, place a pot over medium-high heat, add all the ingredients for the sauce, whisk well until combined and bring to a slight boil.
- Then reduce heat to medium-low level, simmer sauce for 10 minutes and set aside.
- Then place chicken wings in a bowl, add salt and toss until seasoned.
- Switch on the instant pot, place chicken wings in it and pour the prepared sauce over them.
- Press the 'keep warm' button, shut the instant pot with its lid in the sealed position, then press the 'manual' button, press '+/-' to set the cooking time to 10 minutes and cook at high-pressure setting; when the pressure builds in the pot, the cooking timer will start.
- Meanwhile, switch on the broiler and let it preheat.
- When the instant pot buzzes, press the 'keep warm' button, do a quick pressure release and open the lid.
- Transfer chicken to a baking sheet, brush both sides of the chicken wings with sauce from the instant pot and then broil for 10 minutes or until glazed, flipping chicken wings halfway through.
- Serve straight away.

Nutritional Info:

Calories: 304; Fat: 21 g; Protein: 27.2 g; Net Carbs: 2.1 g; Fiber: 5.7 g;

Coconut Chicken

Prep Time: 5 minutes; Cooking Time: 22 minutes; Servings: 4;

Ingredients:

- Bunch of celery, chopped – 1
- Chicken breast, cubed – 1 pound
- Chicken broth – 1 cup
- Stalks of lemongrass – 5
- Coconut milk, unsweetened, full-fat – 1 cup
- Salt – ¾ teaspoon
- Ground black pepper – ½ teaspoon

Directions:

- Switch on the instant pot, add celery, then top with chicken, add lemongrass and pour in chicken broth.
- Shut the instant pot with its lid in the sealed position, then press the 'manual' button, press '+/-' to set the cooking time to 22 minutes and cook at high-pressure setting; when the pressure builds in the pot, the cooking timer will start.
- When the instant pot buzzes, press the 'keep warm' button, do a quick pressure release and open the lid.
- Remove and discard lemongrass, season with salt and black pepper, then pour in coconut milk and stir until combined.
- Serve coconut chicken with cauliflower rice.

Nutritional Info:

Calories: 260; Fat: 15.1 g; Protein: 27.8 g; Net Carbs: 1 g; Fiber: 2.2 g;

Buffalo Chicken Meatballs

Prep Time: 10 minutes; Cooking Time: 26 minutes; Servings: 6;

Ingredients:

- Avocado oil – 2 tablespoons
- Hot sauce – 6 tablespoons
- Butter, unsalted – 4 tablespoons
- For Meatballs:
- Ground chicken – 1.5-pound
- Almond meal – 3/4 cup
- Sea salt – 1 teaspoon
- Minced garlic – 1 tablespoon
- Green onions, sliced – 2

Directions:

- Place all the ingredients for the meatballs in a bowl, stir until combined and then shape the mixture into 2-inch wide meatballs.
- Switch on the instant pot, grease pot with oil, press the 'sauté/simmer' button, wait until the oil is hot, add meatballs in a single layer and cook for 3 minutes or more until nicely browned.
- Meanwhile, place butter and hot sauce in a heatproof bowl, microwave for 1 minute or until the butter completely melts, then whisk until smooth and set aside.
- Transfer meatballs to a plate, cook remaining meatballs in the same manner, then stack meatballs in the instant pot and pour prepared sauce over them.
- Press the 'keep warm' button, shut the instant pot with its lid in the sealed position, then press the 'manual' button, press

'+/-' to set the cooking time to 20 minutes and cook at high-pressure setting; when the pressure builds in the pot, the cooking timer will start.
- When the instant pot buzzes, press the 'keep warm' button, do a quick pressure release and open the lid.
- Serve meatballs with zucchini noodles.

Nutritional Info:

Calories: 357; Fat: 28 g; Protein: 23 g; Net Carbs: 2 g; Fiber: 1 g;

Tomatillo Chili

Prep Time: 5 minutes; Cooking Time: 45 minutes; Servings: 8;

Ingredients:

- Ground beef – 1 pound
- Ground pork – 1 pound
- Tomatillos, chopped – 3
- White onion, peeled and chopped – ½
- Tomato paste – 6 ounces
- Garlic powder – 1 teaspoon
- Jalapeno pepper, chopped – 1
- Ground cumin – 1 tablespoon
- Red chili powder – 1 tablespoon
- Water – 1 cup
- Salt – 1 ½ teaspoon
- Parmesan cheese, grated – 1 cup

Directions:

- Switch on the instant pot, grease pot with oil, press the 'sauté/simmer' button, wait until the oil is hot, add ground beef and pork and cook for 5 minutes or more until nicely browned.
- Add remaining ingredients into the instant pot except for cheese, stir well and press the 'keep warm' button.
- Shut the instant pot with its lid in the sealed position, then press the 'manual' button, press '+/-' to the set the cooking time to 35 minutes and cook at high-pressure setting; when the pressure builds in the pot, the cooking timer will start.
- When the instant pot buzzes, press the 'keep warm' button, release pressure naturally for 10 minutes, then do a quick pressure release and open the lid.
- Ladle chili into bowls, top with parmesan cheese and serve.

Nutritional Info:

Calories: 325; Fat: 23 g; Protein: 20 g; Net Carbs: 5 g; Fiber: 1 g;

Garlic Chicken

Prep Time: 5 minutes; Cooking Time: 35 minutes; Servings: 4;

Ingredients:

- Chicken breasts – 4
- Salt – 1 teaspoon
- Avocado oil – ¼ cup
- Turmeric powder – 1 teaspoon
- Cloves of garlic, peeled and diced – 10

Directions:

- Switch on the instant pot, add chicken, then season with salt and black pepper, pour in the oil and scatter garlic on top.
- Shut the instant pot with its lid in the sealed position, then press the 'manual' button, press '+/-' to set the cooking time to 35 minutes and cook at high-pressure setting; when the pressure builds in the pot, the cooking timer will start.
- When the instant pot buzzes, press the 'keep warm' button, release pressure naturally for 10 minutes, then do a quick pressure release and open the lid.
- Shred chicken with two forks, toss until mixed and serve as a lettuce wrap.

Nutritional Info:

Calories: 404; Fat: 21 g; Protein: 47 g; Net Carbs: 3 g; Fiber: 0 g;

Soups & Stews

Cream Zucchini Soup

Prep Time: 8-10 min.

Cooking Time: 8 min.

Number of Servings: 4

Ingredients:

- 2 cups vegetable stock
- 2 garlic cloves, crushed
- 1 tablespoon butter
- 4 (preferably medium size) zucchinis, peeled and chopped
- 1 small onion, chopped
- 2 cups heavy cream
- 1/2 teaspoon dried oregano, (finely ground)
- 1/2 teaspoon black pepper, (finely ground)
- 1 teaspoon dried parsley, (finely ground)
- 1 teaspoon of sea salt
- Lemon juice (optional)

Directions:

1. Arrange Instant Pot over a dry platform in your kitchen. Open its top lid and switch it on.
2. Find and press "SAUTE" cooking function; add the butter in it and allow it to melt.

3. In the pot, add the onions, zucchini, garlic; cook (while stirring) until turns translucent and softened for around 2-3 minutes.
4. Add the vegetable broth and sprinkle with salt, oregano, pepper, and parsley; gently stir to mix well.
5. Close the lid to create a locked chamber; make sure that safety valve is in locking position.
6. Find and press "MANUAL" cooking function; timer to 5 minutes with default "HIGH" pressure mode.
7. Allow the pressure to build to cook the ingredients.
8. After cooking time is over press "CANCEL" setting. Find and press "QPR" cooking function. This setting is for quick release of inside pressure.
9. Slowly open the lid, take out the cooked recipe in serving plates or serving bowls, and enjoy the keto recipe. Top with some lemon juice.

Nutritional Values (Per Serving):

Calories – 264; Fat – 26g; Saturated Fat – 7g; Trans Fat – 0g; Carbohydrates – 11g; Fiber – 3g; Sodium – 564mg; Protein – 4g

Coconut Chicken Soup

Prep Time: 8-10 min.

Cooking Time: 18 min.

Number of Servings: 4

Ingredients:

- 4 cloves of garlic, minced

- 1 pound chicken breasts, skin-on
- 4 cups of water
- 2 tablespoons olive oil
- 1 onion, diced
- 1 cup of coconut milk
- (finely ground) black pepper and salt as per taste preference
- 2 tablespoons sesame oil

Directions:

1. Arrange Instant Pot over a dry platform in your kitchen. Open its top lid and switch it on.
2. Find and press "SAUTE" cooking function; add the oil in it and allow it to heat.
3. In the pot, add the onions, garlic; cook (while stirring) until turns translucent and softened for around 1-2 minutes.
4. Stir in the chicken breasts; stir, and cook for 2 more minutes.
5. Pour in water and coconut milk — season to taste.
6. Close the lid to create a locked chamber; make sure that safety valve is in locking position.
7. Find and press "MANUAL" cooking function; timer to 15 minutes with default "HIGH" pressure mode.
8. Allow the pressure to build to cook the ingredients.
9. After cooking time is over press "CANCEL" setting. Find and press "NPR" cooking function. This setting is for the natural release of inside pressure and it takes around 10 minutes to slowly release pressure.
10. Slowly open the lid, Drizzle with sesame oil on top.
11. Take out the cooked recipe in serving plates or serving bowls and enjoy the keto recipe.

Nutritional Values (Per Serving):

Calories – 328; Fat – 31g; Saturated Fat – 6g; Trans Fat – 0g; Carbohydrates – 6g; Fiber – 4g; Sodium – 76mg; Protein – 21g.

Chicken Bacon Soup

Prep Time: 8-10 min.

Cooking Time: 40 min.

Number of Servings: 4

Ingredients:

- 6 boneless, skinless chicken thighs, make cubes
- ½ cup chopped celery
- 4 minced garlic cloves
- 6-ounce mushrooms, sliced
- ½ cup chopped onion
- 8-ounce softened cream cheese
- ¼ cup softened butter
- 1 teaspoon dried thyme
- Salt and (finely ground) black pepper, as per taste preference
- 2 cups chopped spinach
- 8 ounces cooked bacon slices, chopped
- 3 cups (preferably homemade) chicken broth
- 1 cup heavy cream

Directions:

1. Arrange Instant Pot over a dry platform in your kitchen. Open its top lid and switch it on.
2. Add the ingredients except for the cream, spinach, and bacon; gently stir to mix well.
3. Close the lid to create a locked chamber; make sure that safety valve is in locking position.
4. Find and press "SOUP" cooking function; timer to 30 minutes with default "HIGH" pressure mode.
5. Allow the pressure to build to cook the ingredients.
6. After cooking time is over press "CANCEL" setting. Find and press "NPR" cooking function. This setting is for the natural release of inside pressure and it takes around 10 minutes to slowly release pressure.
7. Slowly open the lid, stir in cream and spinach.
8. Take out the cooked recipe in serving plates or serving bowls and enjoy the keto recipe. Top with the bacon.

Nutritional Values (Per Serving):

Calories – 456; Fat – 38g; Saturated Fat – 13g; Trans Fat – 0g; Carbohydrates – 7g; Fiber – 1g; Sodium – 742mg; Protein – 23g.

Cream Pepper Stew

Prep Time: 8-10 min.

Cooking Time: 10 min.

Number of Servings: 4

Ingredients:

- 1 (preferably medium size) celery stalk, chopped
- 1 (preferably medium size) yellow bell pepper, chopped
- 1 (preferably medium size) green bell pepper, chopped
- 2 large red bell peppers, chopped
- 1 small red onion, chopped
- 2 tablespoons butter
- 1/2 cup cream cheese, full-fat
- 1/4 teaspoon dried thyme, (finely ground)
- 1/2 teaspoon black pepper, (finely ground)
- 1 teaspoon dried parsley, (finely ground)
- 1 teaspoon salt
- 2 cups vegetable stock
- 1 cup heavy cream

Directions:

1. Arrange Instant Pot over a dry platform in your kitchen. Open its top lid and switch it on.
2. Find and press "SAUTE" cooking function; add the butter in it and allow it to heat.
3. In the pot, add the onions, bell pepper, and celery; cook (while stirring) until turns translucent and softened for around 3-4 minutes.
4. Pour in the vegetable stock and heavy cream — season with salt, pepper, parsley, and thyme.
5. Close the lid to create a locked chamber; make sure that safety valve is in locking position.
6. Find and press "MANUAL" cooking function; timer to 6 minutes with default "HIGH" pressure mode.
7. Allow the pressure to build to cook the ingredients.

8. After cooking time is over press "CANCEL" setting. Find and press "QPR" cooking function. This setting is for quick release of inside pressure.
9. Slowly open the lid, mix in the cream; take out the cooked recipe in serving plates or serving bowls, and enjoy the keto recipe.

Nutritional Values (Per Serving):

Calories – 286; Fat – 27g; Saturated Fat – 6g; Trans Fat – 0g; Carbohydrates – 9g; Fiber – 3g; Sodium – 523mg; Protein – 5g.

Ham Asparagus Soup

Prep Time: 8-10 min.

Cooking Time: 55 min.

Number of Servings: 3-4

Ingredients:

- 5 crushed garlic cloves
- 1 cup chopped ham
- 4 cups (preferably homemade) chicken broth
- 2 pounds trimmed and halved asparagus spears
- 2 tablespoons butter
- 1 chopped yellow onion
- ½ teaspoon dried thyme
- Salt and freshly (finely ground) black pepper, as per taste preference

Directions:

1. Arrange Instant Pot over a dry platform in your kitchen. Open its top lid and switch it on.
2. Find and press "SAUTE" cooking function; add the butter in it and allow it to heat.
3. In the pot, add the onions; cook (while stirring) until turns translucent and softened for around 4-5 minutes.
4. Add the garlic, ham bone and broth; stir, and cook for about 2-3 minutes.
5. Add the other ingredients; gently stir to mix well.
6. Close the lid to create a locked chamber; make sure that safety valve is in locking position.
7. Find and press "SOUP" cooking function; timer to 45 minutes with default "HIGH" pressure mode.
8. Allow the pressure to build to cook the ingredients.
9. After cooking time is over press "CANCEL" setting. Find and press "QPR" cooking function. This setting is for quick release of inside pressure.
10. Slowly open the lid, add the prepared recipe mix in a blender or processor.
11. Blend or process to make a smooth mix. Place the mix in serving bowls and enjoy the keto recipe.

Nutritional Values (Per Serving):

Calories – 146; Fat – 7g; Saturated Fat – 3g; Trans Fat – 0g; Carbohydrates – 5g; Fiber – 4g; Sodium – 262mg; Protein – 10g.

Beef Zoodle Soup

Prep Time: 5 minutes; Cooking Time: 13 minutes; Servings: 4;

Ingredients:

- Avocado oil – 4 tablespoons
- Minced ginger – 3 tablespoons
- Minced garlic – 1 tablespoon
- Sirloin steak tips, cut into 1-inch pieces – 1 ½ pound
- Broccoli florets – 2 cups
- Bella mushrooms, sliced – 8 ounces
- Beef broth – 6 cups
- Apple cider vinegar – 1/4 cup
- Coconut aminos – 1/4 cup
- Sriracha sauce – 1/4 cup
- large zucchini, spiralized into noodles – 1

Directions:

- Switch on the instant pot, grease pot with oil, press the 'sauté/simmer' button, wait until the oil is hot and add the steak pieces along with ginger and garlic.
- Cook steak for 5 minutes or more until nicely golden brown, then add remaining ingredients except for zucchini and stir until mixed.
- Press the 'keep warm' button, shut the instant pot with its lid in the sealed position, then press the 'manual' button, press '+/-' to set the cooking time to 8 minutes and cook at high-pressure setting; when the pressure builds in the pot, the cooking timer will start.
- When the instant pot buzzes, press the 'keep warm' button, do a quick pressure release and open the lid.
- Taste the soup to adjust seasoning, add zucchini noodles and toss until just mixed.
- Ladle the soup into bowls and serve.

Nutritional Info:

Calories: 239; Fat: 11 g; Protein: 29 g; Net Carbs: 3 g; Fiber: 2 g;

Broccoli Cheese Soup

Prep Time: 10 minutes; Cooking Time: 12 minutes; Servings: 5;

Ingredients:

- Butter, unsalted – 2 tablespoons
- Minced garlic – 2 tablespoons
- Vegetable broth – 3 cups
- Broccoli florets – 6-ounce
- Monterey jack cheese, shredded – 1 cup
- Sharp cheddar cheese, shredded – 2 cups, and 2 tablespoons
- Dijon mustard – 1 tablespoon
- Paprika – ½ teaspoon
- Ground black pepper – ⅛ teaspoon
- Heavy whipping cream – 1 cup
- Salt – ¼ teaspoon
- Xanthan gum – 1 teaspoon

Directions:

- Switch on the instant pot, add butter, press the 'sauté/simmer' button, wait until the butter melts and add garlic and cook for 1 minute or until fragrant.
- Stir in broth, cook for 1 minute, then add broccoli florets and stir until mixed.
- Press the 'keep warm' button, shut the instant pot with its lid in the sealed position, then press the 'manual' button, press '+/-' to set the cooking time to 10 minutes and cook at high-pressure setting; when the pressure builds in the pot, the cooking timer will start.
- When the instant pot buzzes, press the 'keep warm' button, do quick pressure release and open the lid.

- Add mustard, Monterey jack cheese, and 2 cups of cheddar cheese, season with black pepper and paprika and stir until cheese begins to melt.
- Then pour in the cream, stir until well-incorporated and taste to adjust salt.
- Take out ¾ cup of soup, add xanthan gum, stir well, then add into the soup in the instant pot and stir well until well combined.
- Garnish soup with remaining cheddar cheese and serve.

Nutritional Info:

Calories: 276; Fat: 23.8 g; Protein: 11.8 g; Net Carbs: 5.1 g; Fiber: 2.7 g;

Zuppa Toscana

Prep Time: 10 minutes; Cooking Time: 25 minutes; Servings: 4;

Ingredients:

- Slices of bacon, chopped – 6
- Ground Italian sausage – 1 pound
- Butter, unsalted – 1 tablespoon
- Minced garlic – 2 teaspoons
- Ground sage – ½ teaspoon
- Ground black pepper – ¼ teaspoon
- Chicken broth – 2 ¾ cups
- Heavy whipping cream – ¾ cup
- Parmesan cheese, shredded – ¼ cup
- Radishes, peeled, quartered – 1 pound
- Kale, de-stemmed, leaves chopped – 2 ounces

Directions:

- Switch on the instant pot, grease pot with oil, press the 'sauté/simmer' button, wait until the oil is hot, add sausage and cook for 5 minutes or until browned.
- Transfer sausage to a plate, add bacon in the pot and cook for 4 minutes or until crispy.
- Transfer bacon to a cutting board, let sit for 5 minutes and then chop it.
- Add garlic in the instant pot, cook for 1 minute or until fragrant, then return sausage and bacon into the pot, add remaining ingredients except for cream, cheese, and kale and stir until mixed.
- Press the 'keep warm' button, shut the instant pot with its lid in the sealed position, then press the 'manual' button, press '+/-' to set the cooking time to 10 minutes and cook at high-pressure setting; when the pressure builds in the pot, the cooking timer will start.
- When the instant pot buzzes, press the 'keep warm' button, do a quick pressure release and open the lid.
- Add remaining ingredients, stir well, press the 'sauté/simmer' button and simmer the soup for 5 minutes or until kale is tender.
- Ladle soup into bowls and serve.

Nutritional Info:

Calories: 316; Fat: 25 g; Protein: 13 g; Net Carbs: 6 g; Fiber: 3 g;

Thai Shrimp Soup

Prep Time: 5 minutes; Cooking Time: 25 minutes; Servings: 6;

Ingredients:

- Butter, unsalted – 2 tablespoons
- Medium shrimp, uncooked, peeled and deveined – ½ pound
- White onion, peeled and diced – ½
- Minced garlic – 1 tablespoon
- Chicken broth – 4 cups
- Lime juice – 2 tablespoons
- Fish sauce – 2 tablespoons
- Red curry paste – 2½ teaspoon
- Coconut aminos – 1 tablespoon
- Stalk of lemongrass, chopped – 1
- Sliced fresh white mushrooms – 1 cup
- Grated ginger – 1 tablespoon
- Sea salt – 1 teaspoon
- Ground black pepper – ½ teaspoon
- Coconut milk, unsweetened, full-fat – 13.66-ounce
- Chopped fresh cilantro – 3 tablespoons

Directions:

- Switch on the instant pot, add 1 tablespoon butter, press the 'sauté/simmer' button, wait until butter melts, add shrimps, stir well and cook for 3 to 5 minutes or until shrimps turn pink.
- Transfer shrimps to a plate, add remaining butter and when it melts, add onion and garlic and cook for 3 minutes.
- Add remaining ingredients, reserving coconut milk, shrimps and cilantro, stir until mixed and press the 'keep warm' button.
- Shut the instant pot with its lid in the sealed position, then press the 'manual' button, press '+/-' to set the cooking time to 5 minutes and cook at high-pressure setting; when the pressure builds in the pot, the cooking timer will start.
- When the instant pot buzzes, press the 'keep warm' button, release pressure naturally for 5 minutes, then do a quick pressure release and open the lid.

- Return shrimps into the instant pot, pour in milk, then press the 'sauté/simmer' button and bring the soup to boil.
- Press the 'keep warm' button, let soup rest for 2 minutes and then ladle soup into bowls.
- Garnish the soup with cilantro and serve.

Nutritional Info:

Calories: 200; Fat: 13 g; Protein: 15 g; Net Carbs: 4 g; Fiber: 1 g;

Chicken and Vegetable Soup

Prep Time: 5 minutes; Cooking Time: 10 minutes; Servings: 4;

Ingredients:

- Butter, unsalted – 4 tablespoons
- White onion, peeled and diced – 1/2 cup
- Carrots, peeled and sliced – 1 cup
- Stalks of celery, sliced – 2
- Minced garlic – 1 ½ tablespoon
- Chicken broth – 8 cups
- Chicken thighs, skinless, boneless – 6
- Fresh dill – 2 teaspoons
- Fresh thyme – 2 teaspoons
- Salt – 1 ½ teaspoon
- Ground black pepper – 1 teaspoon
- Avocado oil – 2 tablespoons

Directions:

- Switch on the instant pot, add butter, press the 'sauté/simmer' button, wait until the oil is hot and add the onion, carrot, celery, and garlic and cook for 5 minutes or until sautéd.
- Meanwhile, prepare the chicken and for this, cut chicken into bite-size pieces.
- Add chicken into vegetables along with remaining ingredients, reserving the oil, and stir until just mixed.
- Press the 'keep warm' button, shut the instant pot with its lid in the sealed position, then press the 'manual' button, press '+/-' to set the cooking time to 4 minutes and cook at high-pressure setting; when the pressure builds in the pot, the cooking timer will start.
- When the instant pot buzzes, press the 'keep warm' button, release pressure naturally for 10 minutes, then do a quick pressure release and open the lid.
- Ladle the soup into bowls, drizzle with oil and serve.

Nutritional Info:

Calories: 330; Fat: 21 g; Protein: 26 g; Net Carbs: 6 g; Fiber: 2 g;

Buffalo Ranch Chicken Dip

Prep Time: 5 minutes; Cooking Time: 15 minutes; Servings: 4;

Ingredients:

- Chicken breast – 1 pound
- Packet of ranch dip – 1
- Hot sauce – 1 cup
- Stick of butter, unsalted – 1
- Cheddar cheese, grated – 16 ounces
- Cream cheese – 8 ounces

Directions:

- Switch on the instant pot and place all the ingredients except for cheddar cheese.
- Shut the instant pot with its lid in the sealed position, then press the 'manual' button, press '+/-' to set the cooking time to 15 minutes and cook at high-pressure setting; when the pressure builds in the pot, the cooking timer will start.
- When the instant pot buzzes, press the 'keep warm' button, do quick pressure release and open the lid.
- Shred chicken with two forks, then add cheddar cheese and stir well until cheese completely melts.
- Serve with vegetable sticks.

Nutritional Info:

Calories: 526; Fat: 40.5 g; Protein: 37 g; Net Carbs: 2.5 g; Fiber: 0.5 g;

Creamy Taco Soup

Prep Time: 5 minutes; Cooking Time: 10 minutes; Servings: 6;

Ingredients:

- Ground beef – 2 pounds
- Minced garlic – 2 tablespoons
- Red chili powder – 2 tablespoons
- Cumin – 2 teaspoons
- Diced tomatoes with chilies – 20 ounces
- Beef broth – 32 ounces
- Salt – 1 ½ teaspoon
- Ground black pepper – ¾ teaspoon

- Cream cheese – 8 ounces
- Heavy cream – 1/2 cup

Directions:

- Switch on the instant pot, press the 'sauté/simmer' button, wait until the pot is hot, then add ground beef and cook for 5 minutes or more until nicely browned.
- Add remaining ingredients except for cream cheese, stir until mixed, then press the 'keep warm' button and shut the instant pot with its lid in the sealed position.
- Press the 'soup' button, press '+/-' to set the cooking time to 5 minutes and cook at high-pressure setting; when the pressure builds in the pot, the cooking timer will start.
- When the instant pot buzzes, press the 'keep warm' button, release pressure naturally for 10 minutes, then do a quick pressure release and open the lid.
- Add cream cheese, stir well until combined and serve.

Nutritional Info:

Calories: 386; Fat: 28 g; Protein: 27 g; Net Carbs: 7 g; Fiber: 1 g;

Chicken Kale Soup

Prep Time: 10 minutes; Cooking Time: 25 minutes; Servings: 4;

Ingredients:

- Baby kale leaves – 5 ounces
- Chicken breast, cubed – 2 pounds
- Sliced white onion – 1/3 cup
- Salt – 1 teaspoon

- Avocado oil – ½ cup and 1 tablespoon
- Chicken broth – 14 ounces
- Chicken stock – 32 ounces
- Lemon juice – 1/4 cup

Directions:

- Switch on the instant pot, grease pot with 1 tablespoon oil, press the 'sauté/simmer' button, and wait until the oil is hot.
- Sprinkle chicken with salt and black pepper until seasoned well, then add into the instant pot and cook for 3 to 5 minutes or until browned on all sides.
- Press the 'keep warm' button, shut the instant pot with its lid in the sealed position and let it sit for 15 minutes or until the internal temperature of chicken reach to 165 degrees F.
- Meanwhile, pour chicken broth in a blender, add onion and remaining oil and pulse until smooth.
- Open the lid of the instant pot, shred chicken with two forks, pour in onion mixture along with remaining ingredients, stir well and shut with lid.
- Press the 'manual' button, press '+/-' to set the cooking time to 10 minutes and cook at high-pressure setting; when the pressure builds in the pot, the cooking timer will start.
- When the instant pot buzzes, press the 'keep warm' button, release pressure naturally for 10 minutes, then do a quick pressure release and open the lid.
- Ladle soup into bowls and serve.

Nutritional Info:

Calories: 261; Fat: 21 g; Protein: 14.1 g; Net Carbs: 1.2 g; Fiber: 0.8 g;

Chicken Thigh Soup

Prep Time: 5 minutes; Cooking Time: 30 minutes; Servings: 6;

Ingredients:

- Chicken thighs, with skin and bones – 2 pounds
- Stalks of celery, chopped – 4
- Radishes, peeled and chopped – 0.65 pounds
- Small white onion, peeled and chopped – 1/2
- Rosemary, chopped – 1 tablespoon
- Basil, chopped – 1 tablespoon
- Minced garlic – 1 tablespoon
- Salt – 1/2 teaspoon
- Ground black pepper – 1/4 teaspoon
- Chicken broth – 4 cups
- Bay leaves – 2

Directions:

- Switch on the instant pot and place all the ingredients in it, with chicken thighs in the end.
- Shut the instant pot with its lid in the sealed position, then press the 'soup' button, press '+/-' to set the cooking time to 30 minutes and cook at high-pressure setting; when the pressure builds in the pot, the cooking timer will start.
- When the instant pot buzzes, press the 'keep warm' button, release pressure naturally and open the lid.
- Transfer chicken thighs to a cutting board, separate its meat from th3 skin and bones, then cut the chicken into bite-sized pieces and return into the soup.
- Taste soup to adjust seasoning, then ladle into bowls and serve.

Nutritional Info:

Calories: 356; Fat: 25 g; Protein: 25 g; Net Carbs: 3 g; Fiber: 1 g;

Dessert

Almond Mug Cake

Prep Time: 8-10 min.

Cooking Time: 10 min.

Number of Servings: 1

Ingredients:

- 1/4 teaspoon baking powder
- 1/4 teaspoon vanilla extract
- 1 1/2 tablespoons cacao powder
- 1 egg, beaten
- 1/4 cup almond flour
- 1 teaspoon cinnamon powder
- 2 tablespoons stevia powder
- A pinch of salt

Directions:

1. Combine all ingredients in the bowl until well-combined. Add the mix in a heat-proof mug; cover with a foil.
2. Arrange Instant Pot over a dry platform in your kitchen. Open its top lid and switch it on.
3. In the pot, pour water. Arrange a trivet or steamer basket inside that came with Instant Pot. Now place/arrange the mug over the trivet/basket.
4. Close the lid to create a locked chamber; make sure that safety valve is in locking position.

5. Find and press "MANUAL" cooking function; timer to 10 minutes with default "HIGH" pressure mode.
6. Allow the pressure to build to cook the ingredients.
7. After cooking time is over press "CANCEL" setting. Find and press "QPR" cooking function. This setting is for quick release of inside pressure.
8. Slowly open the lid, cool down the mug, and serve warm.

Nutritional Values (Per Serving):

Calories – 138; Fat – 13g; Saturated Fat – 6g; Trans Fat – 0g; Carbohydrates – 7g; Fiber – 3g; Sodium – 73mg; Protein – 9g.

Tapioca Keto Pudding

Prep Time: 8-10 min.

Cooking Time: 20 min.

Number of Servings: 4

Ingredients:

- 1 tablespoon Erythritol
- 1 teaspoon chia seeds
- 1 tablespoon tapioca
- 1 tablespoon butter
- 2 cup heavy cream
- 1/4 cup raspberries or strawberries, mashed

Directions:

1. Arrange Instant Pot over a dry platform in your kitchen. Open its top lid and switch it on.
2. Find and press "SAUTE" cooking function.
3. In the pot, add the cream; cook (while stirring) for 4-5 minutes.
4. Add the tapioca and stir it well. Add the Erythritol and butter.
5. In a bowl, mix the chia seeds and berries.
6. Add the berry mix in the pot and stir well.
7. Close the lid to create a locked chamber; make sure that safety valve is in locking position.
8. Find and press "MANUAL" cooking function; timer to 15 minutes with default "HIGH" pressure mode.
9. Allow the pressure to build to cook the ingredients.
10. After cooking time is over press "CANCEL" setting. Find and press "QPR" cooking function. This setting is for quick release of inside pressure.
11. Add in serving bowls, cool down and place in the fridge for 2 hours.
12. Serve chilled.

Nutritional Values (Per Serving):

Calories - 246

Fat – 24g

Saturated Fat – 9g

Trans Fat – 0g

Carbohydrates – 10g

Fiber – 2g

Sodium – 183mg

Protein – 3g

Cream Chocolate Delight

Prep Time: 8-10 min.

Cooking Time: 15 min.

Number of Servings: 4

Ingredients:

- 1 teaspoon orange zest
- 1 teaspoon stevia powder
- 2 heavy cream
- ¼ cup unsweetened dark chocolate, chopped
- 3 eggs
- 1 teaspoon vanilla extract
- ½ teaspoon salt

Directions:

1. Arrange Instant Pot over a dry platform in your kitchen. Open its top lid and switch it on.
2. Find and press "SAUTE" cooking function.
3. In the pot, add the heavy cream, chopped chocolate, stevia powder, vanilla extract, orange zest, and salt; cook (while stirring) until the chocolate is melted.
4. Crack eggs in the pot; stirring constantly. Remove from the instant pot. Add the mixture to 4 mason jars with loose lids.
5. In the pot, pour water. Arrange a trivet or steamer basket inside that came with Instant Pot. Now place/arrange the jars over the trivet/basket.
6. Close the lid to create a locked chamber; make sure that safety valve is in locking position.

7. Find and press "MANUAL" cooking function; timer to 10 minutes with default "HIGH" pressure mode.
8. Allow the pressure to build to cook the ingredients.
9. After cooking time is over press "CANCEL" setting. Find and press "QPR" cooking function. This setting is for quick release of inside pressure.
10. Slowly open the lid, cool down the jars, and chill in the fridge. Serve chilled.

Nutritional Values (Per Serving):

Calories – 254

Fat – 26g

Saturated Fat – 12g

Trans Fat – 0g

Carbohydrates – 5g

Fiber – 1g

Sodium – 168mg

Protein – 8g

Coconut Keto Pudding

Prep Time: 8-10 min.

Cooking Time: 5 min.

Number of Servings: 4

Ingredients:

- 3 tablespoons Stevia granular
- 1/2 teaspoon vanilla extract
- 1 2/3 cup coconut milk
- 3 egg yolks
- 1 tablespoon gelatin

Directions:

1. Arrange Instant Pot over a dry platform in your kitchen. Open its top lid and switch it on.
2. Add the coconut milk.
3. Close the lid to create a locked chamber; make sure that safety valve is in locking position.
4. Find and press "MANUAL" cooking function; timer to 5 minutes with default "HIGH" pressure mode.
5. Allow the pressure to build to cook the ingredients.
6. After cooking time is over press "CANCEL" setting. Find and press "QPR" cooking function. This setting is for quick release of inside pressure.
7. Place the coconut milk in the Instant Pot. Close the lid and make sure that the steam release valve is set to "Sealing."
8. Whisk in egg yolks and the rest of the ingredients.
9. Find and press "SAUTE" cooking function. Cook until boiling the mix.
10. Add in serving bowls, cool down and place in the fridge for 2 hours.
11. Serve chilled.

Nutritional Values (Per Serving):

Calories – 246

Fat – 27g

Saturated Fat – 8g

Trans Fat – 0g

Carbohydrates – 7g

Fiber – 4g

Sodium – 89mg

Protein – 4g

Vanilla Cream Delight

Prep Time: 8-10 min.

Cooking Time: 15 min.

Number of Servings: 4

Ingredients:

- 1 ½ cup heavy cream
- 1 teaspoon vanilla extract
- 8 large eggs
- ¾ cup unsweetened almond milk
- 1 vanilla bean
- 4 tablespoons stevia granular

Directions:

1. Cut the vanilla bean lengthwise using a knife and take out the seeds. Add in a mixing bowl.
2. Mix in the remaining ingredients. Whisk the mix thoroughly and add into four ramekins.

3. Arrange Instant Pot over a dry platform in your kitchen. Open its top lid and switch it on.
4. In the pot, pour 2 cups water. Arrange a trivet or steamer basket inside that came with Instant Pot. Now place/arrange the ramekins over the trivet/basket.
5. Close the lid to create a locked chamber; make sure that safety valve is in locking position.
6. Find and press "MANUAL" cooking function; timer to 15 minutes with default "HIGH" pressure mode.
7. Allow the pressure to build to cook the ingredients.
8. After cooking time is over press "CANCEL" setting. Find and press "QPR" cooking function. This setting is for quick release of inside pressure.
9. Slowly open the lid, cool down the ramekins.
10. Chill in fridge and serve.

Nutritional Values (Per Serving):

Calories - 318

Fat – 26g

Saturated Fat – 7g

Trans Fat – 0g

Carbohydrates – 3g

Fiber – 0g

Sodium – 106mg

Protein – 13g

Orange Custard Cups

Prep Time: 4 hours and 20 minutes; Cooking Time: 5 minutes; Servings: 5;

Ingredients:

- Coconut milk, full-fat – 3 cups
- Eggs – 2
- Fresh orange juice – ¼ cup
- Medium orange, zested – 1
- Keto collagen, grass-fed – 3 scoops
- Vanilla extract, unsweetened – 2 teaspoons
- Erythritol sweetener – 1/8 teaspoon
- Salt – 1/16 teaspoon
- Gelatin, pastured – 1 ½ scoop
- Water – 1 cup

Directions:

- Place all the ingredients in a food processor except for the gelatin and water, pulse until smooth, then add gelatin and blend until smooth.
- Divide the custard evenly between five half-pint jars and cover with their lid.
- Switch on the instant pot, pour in water, insert trivet stand, place jars on it and shut the instant pot with its lid in the sealed position.
- Press the 'manual' button, press '+/-' to the set the cooking time to 5 minutes and cook at high-pressure setting; when the pressure builds in the pot, the cooking timer will start.
- When the instant pot buzzes, press the 'keep warm' button, do a quick pressure release and open the lid.
- Carefully remove the jars, let them cool at room temperature for 15 minutes or more until they can be comfortably picked up.
- Then transfer the custard jars into the refrigerator for a minimum of 4 hours and cool completely.

- When ready to serve, shake the jars a few times to mix all the ingredients and then serve.

Nutritional Info:

Calories: 250; Fat: 24 g; Protein: 5 g; Net Carbs: 2 g; Fiber: 3 g;

Key Lime Curd

Prep Time: 4 hours and 30 minutes; Cooking Time: 10 minutes; Servings: 3;

Ingredients:

- Butter, unsalted – 3 ounces
- Erythritol sweetener – 1 cup
- Eggs – 2
- Egg yolks – 2
- Key lime juice – 2/3 cup
- Key lime zest – 2 teaspoons
- Water – 1 1/2 cups

Directions:

- Place butter in a food processor, add sugar, blend for 2 minutes, then add eggs and yolks and continue blending for 1 minute.
- Add lime juice, blend until combined and a smooth curd comes together and then pour the mixture evenly into three half-pint mason jars.
- Switch on the instant pot, pour in water, insert a trivet stand, place mason jars on it and shut the instant pot with its lid the in the sealed position.

- Press the 'manual' button, press '+/-' to set the cooking time to 10 minutes and cook at high-pressure setting; when the pressure builds in the pot, the cooking timer will start.
- When the instant pot buzzes, press the 'keep warm' button, release pressure naturally for 10 minutes, then do a quick pressure release and open the lid.
- Remove jars from the instant pot, open them, add lime zest, stir until combined and then close the jars with their lids again.
- Let the jars cool at room temperature for 20 minutes, then place them in the refrigerator for 4 hours or more until chilled and curd gets thickened.
- Serve straight away.

Nutritional Info:

Calories: 78; Fat: 4.5 g; Protein: 7 g; Net Carbs: 1 g; Fiber: 1 g;

Thai Coconut Custard

Prep Time: 4 hours and 5 minutes; Cooking Time: 30 minutes; Servings: 4;

Ingredients:

- Coconut milk, full-fat – 1 cup
- Eggs – 3
- Erythritol sweetener – 1/3 cup
- Vanilla extract, unsweetened – 4 drops
- Water – 2 cups

Directions:

- Place all the ingredients in a bowl, except for water, blend until smooth, then pour the mixture into a 6-inch heatproof bowl and cover it with aluminum foil.
- Switch on the instant pot, pour in water, insert trivet stand and place covered bowl on it.
- Shut the instant pot with its lid the in the sealed position, then press the 'manual' button, press '+/-' to set the cooking time to 30 minutes and cook at high-pressure setting; when the pressure builds in the pot, the cooking timer will start.
- When the instant pot buzzes, press the 'keep warm' button, release pressure naturally for 10 minutes, then do a quick pressure release and open the lid.
- Take out the bowl, uncover it, and check if the custard is cooked which can be done by inserting a knife in the custard that should slide out clean.
- Transfer the custard bowl in the refrigerator and then cool for 4 hours before serving.

Nutritional Info:

Calories: 174; Fat: 14 g; Protein: 6 g; Net Carbs: 5 g; Fiber: 0 g;

Molten Brownie Cups

Prep Time: 10 minutes; Cooking Time: 9 minutes; Servings: 4;

Ingredients:

- Chocolate chips, sugar-free – ⅔ cup
- Butter, salted – 6 tablespoons
- Eggs – 3
- Swerve sweetener – ⅔ cup
- Almond flour – 3 ½ tablespoons
- Vanilla extract, unsweetened – 1 teaspoon

- Water – 1 ¾ cups

Directions:

- Take a medium saucepan, place it over medium-low heat, add chocolate chips and butter and cook for 5 minutes or until chocolate and butter melts and is blended, stirring frequently.
- Crack eggs in a bowl, add flour, sweetener, and vanilla, whisk until blended, and then whisk in chocolate mixture until combined.
- Take four 6-ounce ramekins, grease them with avocado oil and then evenly pour in muffin batter until halfway full.
- Switch on the instant pot, pour in water, then insert a trivet stand and stack ramekins on it.
- Shut the instant pot with its lid in the sealed position, then press the 'manual' button, press '+/-' to set the cooking time to 9 minutes and cook at high-pressure setting; when the pressure builds in the pot, the cooking timer will start.
- When the instant pot buzzes, press the 'keep warm' button, do a quick pressure release and open the lid.
- Take out the ramekins, let cool for 10 minutes at room temperature, then garnish with cream and serve.

Nutritional Info:

Calories: 425; Fat: 36 g; Protein: 9 g; Net Carbs: 7 g; Fiber: 3 g;

Chocolate Mousse

Prep Time: 4 hours and 20 minutes; Cooking Time: 6 minutes; Servings: 5;

Ingredients:

- Egg yolks – 4
- Swerve sweetener – 1/2 cup
- Water, divided – 1 3/4 cup
- Cacao powder, unsweetened – 1/4 cup
- Whipping cream – 1 cup
- Almond milk, full-fat – 1/2 cup
- Vanilla extract, unsweetened – 1/2 teaspoon
- Sea salt – 1/4 teaspoon

Directions:

- Take a saucepan, add cacao and sweetener, pour in ¼ cup water, whisk until sugar is dissolved and then whisk in cream and milk until mixed.
- Place the saucepan over medium heat, bring the mixture to a slight boil, then remove the pan from the heat, add salt and vanilla into the milk mixture and whisk well.
- Place egg yolks in a bowl, whisk until beaten, then slowly whisk in chocolate mixture until incorporated and divide the mixture evenly between five ramekins.
- Switch on the instant pot, pour in water, then insert a trivet stand and stack ramekins on it.
- Shut the instant pot with its lid in the sealed position, then press the 'manual' button, press '+/-' to set the cooking time to 6 minutes and cook at high-pressure setting; when the pressure builds in the pot, the cooking timer will start.
- When the instant pot buzzes, press the 'keep warm' button, do a quick pressure release and open the lid.
- Take out the ramekins, let cool for 10 minutes at room temperature, then transfer them into the refrigerator and chill mousse for 4 hours.
- Serve straight away.

Nutritional Info:

Calories: 250; Fat: 26.4 g; Protein: 2.1 g; Net Carbs: 3.5 g; Fiber: 0.6 g;

Spice Cake

Prep Time: 10 minutes; Cooking Time: 50 minutes; Servings: 10;

Ingredients:

- Almond flour – 2 cups
- Erythritol sweetener – ½ cup
- Baking powder – 2 teaspoons
- Ground cinnamon – 1 teaspoon
- Ground ginger – 1 teaspoon
- Ground cloves – ¼ teaspoon
- Salt – ¼ teaspoon
- Eggs – 2
- Butter, unsalted, melted – 1/3 cup
- Water, divided – 1 1/3 cup
- Vanilla extract, unsweetened – ½ teaspoon
- Chopped toasted pecans – 3 tablespoons

Directions:

- Place all the ingredients in a bowl, reserving 1 cup water and pecans, and stir well using a hand mixer until incorporated and a smooth batter comes together.
- Take a 7-inch baking pan, spoon the prepared batter on it, then smooth the top, sprinkle with pecans and cover the pan with aluminum foil.
- Switch on the instant pot, pour in water, insert a trivet stand and place pan on it.
- Shut the instant pot with its lid in the sealed position, then press the 'cake' button, press '+/-' to set the cooking time to 40 minutes and cook at high-pressure setting; when the pressure builds in the pot, the cooking timer will start.

- When the instant pot buzzes, press the 'keep warm' button, release pressure naturally for 10 minutes, then do a quick pressure release and open the lid.
- Take out the pan, uncover it, invert the pan on a plate to take out the cake and let cool for 10 minutes.
- Spread cream on top of the cake, then cut into slices and serve.

Nutritional Info:

Calories: 229; Fat: 21 g; Protein: 6 g; Net Carbs: 2 g; Fiber: 0 g;

Coconut Almond Cake

Prep Time: 10 minutes; Cooking Time: 50 minutes; Servings: 8;

Ingredients:

- Almond flour – 1 cup
- Shredded coconut, unsweetened – 1/2 cup
- Erythritol sweetener – 1/3 cup
- Baking powder – 1 teaspoon
- Apple pie spice – 1 teaspoon
- Eggs, whisked – 2
- Butter, unsalted, melted – 1/4 cup
- Heavy whipping cream – 1/2 cup and more for topping
- Water – 1 cup

Directions:

- Place all the ingredients in a bowl, reserving water, and stir well using a hand mixer until incorporated and a smooth batter comes together.

- Take a 6-inch baking pan, spoon the prepared batter on it, then smooth the top, sprinkle with pecans and cover the pan with aluminum foil.
- Switch on the instant pot, pour in water, insert a trivet stand and place pan on it.
- Shut the instant pot with its lid in the sealed position, then press the 'cake' button, press '+/-' to set the cooking time to 40 minutes and cook at high-pressure setting; when the pressure builds in the pot, the cooking timer will start.
- When the instant pot buzzes, press the 'keep warm' button, release pressure naturally for 10 minutes, then do a quick pressure release and open the lid.
- Take out the pan, uncover it, invert the pan on a plate to take out the cake and let cool for 15 minutes.
- Spread cream on top of the cake, then cut into slices and serve.

Nutritional Info:

Calories: 236; Fat: 23 g; Protein: 5 g; Net Carbs: 3 g; Fiber: 2 g;

Carrot Cake

Prep Time: 10 minutes; Cooking Time: 50 minutes; Servings: 8;

Ingredients:

- Eggs – 3
- Almond flour – 1 cup
- Swerve sweetener – 2/3 cup
- Baking powder – 1 teaspoon
- Apple pie spice – 1 ½ teaspoon
- Avocado oil – 1/4 cup
- Heavy whipping cream – 1/2 cup

- Carrots, shredded – 1 cup
- Walnuts, chopped – 1/2 cup
- Water – 2 cups

Directions:

- Place all the ingredients in a bowl, reserving water, and stir well using a hand mixer until incorporated and a smooth batter comes together.
- Take a 6-inch baking pan, spoon the prepared batter on it, then smooth the top, sprinkle with pecans and cover the pan with aluminum foil.
- Switch on the instant pot, pour in water, insert a trivet stand and place pan on it.
- Shut the instant pot with its lid in the sealed position, then press the 'cake' button, press '+/-' to set the cooking time to 40 minutes and cook at high-pressure setting; when the pressure builds in the pot, the cooking timer will start.
- When the instant pot buzzes, press the 'keep warm' button, release pressure naturally for 10 minutes, then do a quick pressure release and open the lid.
- Take out the pan, uncover it, invert the pan on a plate to take out the cake and let cool for 15 minutes.
- Spread cream on top of the cake, then cut into slices and serve.

Nutritional Info:

Calories: 268; Fat: 25 g; Protein: 6 g; Net Carbs: 4 g; Fiber: 2 g;

Chocolate Avocado Ice Cream

Prep Time: 12 hours and 10 minutes; Cooking Time: 0 minutes; Servings: 6;

Ingredients:

- Large organic avocados, pitted – 2
- Erythritol, powdered – ½ cup
- Cocoa powder, organic and unsweetened – ½ cup
- Drops of liquid stevia – 25
- Vanilla extract, unsweetened – 2 teaspoons
- Coconut milk, full-fat and unsweetened – 1 cup
- Heavy whipping cream, full-fat – ½ cup
- Squares of chocolate, unsweetened and chopped – 6

Directions:

- Scoop out the flesh from each avocado, place it in a bowl and add vanilla, milk, and cream and blend using an immersion blender until smooth and creamy.
- Add remaining ingredients except for chocolate and mix until well combined and smooth.
- Fold in chopped chocolate and let the mixture chill in the refrigerator for 8 to 12 hours or until cooled.
- When ready to serve, let ice cream stand for 30 minutes at room temperature, then process it using an ice cream machine as per manufacturer instruction.
- Serve immediately.

Nutritional Info:

Calories: 216.7; Fat: 19.4 g; Protein: 3.8 g; Net Carbs: 3.7 g; Fiber: 7.4 g;

Mocha Mousse

Prep Time: 2 hours and 35 minutes; Cooking Time: 0 minutes; Servings: 4;

Ingredients:

    For the Cream Cheese:
- Cream cheese, softened and full-fat – 8 ounces
- Sour cream, full-fat – 3 tablespoons
- Butter, softened – 2 tablespoons
- Vanilla extract, unsweetened – 1 ½ teaspoons
- Erythritol – 1/3 cup
- Cocoa powder, unsweetened – ¼ cup
- Instant coffee powder – 3 teaspoons
For the Whipped Cream:
- Heavy whipping cream, full-fat – 2/3 cup
- Erythritol – 1 ½ teaspoon
- Vanilla extract, unsweetened – ½ teaspoon

Directions:

- Prepare cream cheese mixture: For this, place cream cheese in a bowl, add sour cream and butter then beat until smooth.
- Now add erythritol, cocoa powder, coffee, and vanilla and blend until incorporated, set aside until required.
- Prepare whipping cream: For this, place whipping cream in a bowl and beat until soft peaks form.
- Beat in vanilla and erythritol until stiff peaks form, then add 1/3 of the mixture into cream cheese mixture and fold until just mixed.
- Then add remaining whipping cream mixture and fold until evenly incorporated.

- Spoon the mousse into a freezer-proof bowl and place in the refrigerator for 2 ½ hours until set.
- Serve straight away.

Nutritional Info:

Calories: 421.7; Fat: 42 g; Protein: 6 g; Net Carbs: 6.5 g; Fiber: 2 g;

Strawberry Rhubarb Custard

Prep Time: 4 hours and 5 minutes; Cooking Time: 5 minutes; Servings: 5;

Ingredients:

- Coconut milk, full-fat – 27 ounces
- Eggs – 2
- Strawberries, fresh – ¾ cup
- Rhubarb, chopped – ½ cup
- Collagen, grass-fed – ¼ cup
- Vanilla extract, unsweetened – 1 teaspoon
- Stevia, liquid – 1/16 teaspoon
- Salt – 1/16 teaspoon
- Gelatin, grass-fed – 1 ½ tablespoons
- Water – 1 cup

Directions:

- Place all the ingredients in a food processor except for the gelatin and water, pulse until smooth, then add gelatin and blend until smooth.
- Divide the custard evenly between five half-pint jars and cover with their lid.

- Switch on the instant pot, pour in water, insert trivet stand, place jars on it and shut the instant pot with its lid the in the sealed position.
- Press the 'manual' button, press '+/-' to set the cooking time to 5 minutes and cook at high-pressure setting; when the pressure builds in the pot, the cooking timer will start.
- When the instant pot buzzes, press the 'keep warm' button, do a quick pressure release and open the lid.
- Carefully remove the jars, let them cool at room temperature for 15 minutes or more until they can be comfortably picked up.
- Then transfer the custard jars into the refrigerator for a minimum of 4 hours and cool completely.
- When ready to serve, shake the jars a few times to mix all the ingredients and then serve.

Nutritional Info:

Calories: 262; Fat: 24 g; Protein: 5 g; Net Carbs: 3 g; Fiber: 3 g;

Creme Brulee

Prep Time: 4 hours and 25 minutes; Cooking Time: 9 minutes; Servings: 6;

Ingredients:

- Heavy whipping cream – 2 cups
- Egg yolks – 6
- Erythritol sweetener – 5 tablespoons
- Vanilla extract, unsweetened – 1 tablespoon
- Water – 1 cup

Directions:

- Place all the ingredients in a large bowl, reserving 2 tablespoons sweetener and water, and whisk well until combined.
- Evenly divide the mixture among six ramekins and then cover each ramekin with aluminum foil.
- Switch on the instant pot, pour in water, then insert trivet stand and stack ramekins on it.
- Shut the instant pot with its lid in the sealed position, then press the 'manual' button, press '+/-' to the set the cooking time to 9 minutes and cook at high-pressure setting; when the pressure builds in the pot, the cooking timer will start.
- When the instant pot buzzes, press the 'keep warm' button, release pressure naturally for 15 minutes, then do a quick pressure release and open the lid.
- Take out the ramekins, uncover them, let rest for 15 minutes at room temperature and then cool completely in the refrigerator for 4 hours.
- When ready to serve, sprinkle 1 teaspoon of remaining sweetener over each crème Brulee and burn the sweetener by using a hand torch.
- Serve straight away.

Nutritional Info:

Calories: 500; Fat: 51 g; Protein: 6 g; Net Carbs: 5 g; Fiber: 0 g;

Pumpkin Pie Pudding

Prep Time: 4 hours and 25 minutes; Cooking Time: 20 minutes; Servings: 4;

Ingredients:

- Eggs – 2
- Heavy whipping cream, divided – 1 cup
- Erythritol sweetener – 3/4 cup
- Pumpkin puree – 15 ounces
- Pumpkin pie spice – 1 teaspoon
- Vanilla extract, unsweetened – 1 teaspoon
- Water – 1 ½ cup

Directions:

- Crack eggs in a bowl, add ½ cup cream, sweetener, pumpkin puree, pumpkin pie spice, and vanilla and whisk until blended.
- Take a 6 by 3-inch baking pan, grease it well with avocado oil, then pour in egg mixture, smooth the top and cover with aluminum foil.
- Switch on the instant pot, pour in water, insert a trivet stand and place baking pan on it.
- Shut the instant pot with its lid in the sealed position, then press the 'manual' button, press '+/-' to the set the cooking time to 20 minutes and cook at high-pressure setting; when the pressure builds in the pot, the cooking timer will start.
- When the instant pot buzzes, press the 'keep warm' button, release pressure naturally for 10 minutes, then do a quick pressure release and open the lid.
- Take out the baking pan, uncover it, let cool for 15 minutes at room temperature, then transfer the pan into the refrigerator for 4 hours or until cooled.
- Top pie with remaining cream, then cut it into slices and serve.

Nutritional Info:

Calories: 184; Fat: 16 g; Protein: 3 g; Net Carbs: 5 g; Fiber: 2 g;

Chocolate Muffins

Prep Time: 10 minutes; Cooking Time: 30 minutes; Yield: 8 muffins;

Ingredients:

- Pumpkin, chopped, steamed – 2 cups
- Coconut flour – 1/2 cup
- Salt – 1/8 teaspoon
- Erythritol sweetener – 4 tablespoons
- Cacao powder, unsweetened – 1 cup
- Collagen protein powder – 1/2 cup
- Baking soda – 1 teaspoon
- Cacao butter, melted – 4.6 ounces
- Avocado oil – 1/2 cup
- Apple cider vinegar – 2 teaspoons
- Vanilla extract, unsweetened – 3 teaspoons
- Eggs, pastured – 3

Directions:

- Set oven to 350 degrees F and let preheat until muffins are ready to bake.
- Add all the ingredients in a food processor or blender, except for collagen, and pulse for 1 to 2 minutes or until well combined and incorporated.
- Then add collagen and pulse at low speed until just mixed.
- Take an eight cups silicon muffin tray, grease the cups with avocado oil and then evenly scoop the prepared batter in them.
- Place the muffin tray into the oven and bake the muffins for 30 minutes or until thoroughly cooked and a knife inserted into each muffin comes out clean.

- When done, let muffins cool in the pan for 10 minutes, then take them out from the tray and cool on the wire rack.
- Place muffins in a large freezer bag or wrap each muffin with a foil and store them in the refrigerator for four days or in the freezer for up to 3 months.
- When ready to serve, microwave muffins for 45 seconds to 1 minute or until thoroughly heated and then serve with coconut cream.

Nutritional Info:

Calories: 111; Fat: 9.9 g; Protein: 2.8 g; Net Carbs: 3 g; Fiber: 1 g;

Lemon Fat Bombs

Prep Time: 40 minutes; Cooking Time: 0 minutes; Yield: 10 fat bombs;

Ingredients:

- Coconut butter, full-fat – 3/4 cup
- Avocado oil – 1/4 cup
- Lemon juice – 3 tablespoons
- Zest of lemon – 1
- Coconut cream, full-fat – 1 tablespoon
- Erythritol sweetener – 1 tablespoon
- Vanilla extract, unsweetened – 1 teaspoon
- Salt – 1/8 teaspoon

Directions:

- Place all the ingredients for fat bombs in a blender and pulse until well combined.

- Take a baking dish, line it with parchment sheet, then transfer the fat bomb mixture on the sheet and place the sheet into the freezer for 45 minutes until firm enough to shape into balls.
- Then remove the baking sheet from the freezer, roll the fat bomb mixture into ten balls, and arrange the fat bombs on the baking sheet in a single layer.
- Return the baking sheet into the freezer, let chilled until hard and set, and then store in the freezer for up to 2 months.
- Serve when required.

Nutritional Info:

Calories: 164; Fat: 16.7 g; Protein: 1.3 g; Net Carbs: 0.4 g; Fiber: 3 g;

Vanilla Frozen Yogurt

Prep Time: 6 hours and 10 minutes; Cooking Time: 0 minutes; Yield: 8 scoops;

Ingredients:

- Yogurt, organic, full-fat, chilled – 1 cup
- Erythritol sweetener – 4 tablespoons
- MCT oil – 1 tablespoon
- Vanilla extract, unsweetened – 2 teaspoons
- Lime juice – 1 tablespoon

Directions:

- Add all the ingredients in a blender or food processor and pulse for 1 to 2 minutes or until smooth and creamy

- Then pour the yogurt mixture into a large meal prep glass container and store in the freezer for 5 to 6 hours until hard and for up to 3 to 4 months.
- When ready to serve, let yogurt rest at room temperature for 15 to 20 minutes or until slightly soft and then scoop into bowls.

Nutritional Info:

Calories: 122; Fat: 11.4 g; Protein: 3.2 g; Net Carbs: 2.7 g; Fiber: 0 g;

Ice Cream

Prep Time: 6 hours and 10 minutes; Cooking Time: 55 minutes; Yield: 8 scoops;

Ingredients:

- Erythritol sweetener – 1/3 cup
- Butter, grass-fed, unsalted – 3 tablespoons
- MCT oil – 1/4 cup
- Vanilla extract, unsweetened – 1 teaspoon
- Heavy cream, full-fat – 3 cups

Directions:

- Place a large saucepan over medium, add butter and cook for 3 to 5 minutes or until butter melts.
- Add 2 cups cream and sweetener, stir well, bring the mixture to boil, then reduce heat to medium-low level and simmer the mixture for 30 to 45 minutes or until reduced by half and thickened enough to coat the back of a spoon.

- Then pour the ice cream mixture into a large bowl and let it cool at the room temperature.
- Add MCT oil and vanilla, stir until mixed and whisk in remaining cream until smooth.
- Pour the mixture into a large meal prep container, smooth the top with a spatula and let it freeze for 5 to 6 hours or until firm, stirring the ice cream every 30 minutes in the first two hours and every 1 hour for the next 2 to 3 hours.
- Then shut the container with its lid and store the ice cream for 3 to 4 months.
- When ready to serve, let ice cream rest at room temperature for 15 to 20 minutes or until soften and then scoop into bowls.

Nutritional Info:

Calories: 347; Fat: 36 g; Protein: 2 g; Net Carbs: 3 g; Fiber: 0 g;

Custard

Prep Time: 10 minutes; Cooking Time: 45 minutes; Yield: 6 ramekins;

Ingredients:

- Eggs, pastured – 2
- Heavy cream, full-fat – 2 cups
- Erythritol sweetener, powdered – 1/2 cup
- Sea salt – 1/4 teaspoon
- Cinnamon – ½ teaspoon
- Vanilla extract, unsweetened – 2 teaspoons

Directions:

- Set oven to 350 degrees F and let preheat.
- Meanwhile, crack the eggs in a bowl and beat at medium-low speed for 30 seconds or until frothy, set aside until required.
- Place a saucepan over medium-low heat, pour in the cream, sprinkle with salt and sweetener, stir well and cook for 3 to 4 minutes or until small bubbles form on the edges, don't let it boil.
- Stir in vanilla, then very slowly whisk the mixture into eggs, then divide the mixture into six 4-ounces ramekins and sprinkle cinnamon on top.
- Insert ramekins into a deep baking dish and then pour in enough cover until it reaches half of the sides of the ramekins.
- Place the baking dish into the oven and bake for 30 to 40 minutes or until the custard starts to set and a knife slide into custard ramekins comes out clean.
- Carefully remove the custard from the dish, let them cool at room temperature until set and then store in the refrigerator for up to five days.
- Serve straight away.

Nutritional Info:

Calories: 303; Fat: 30 g; Protein: 4 g; Net Carbs: 2 g; Fiber: 0 g;

CONCLUSION

Now that you have made up your mind to start your keto journey, you need to make your experience the best of the best. Therefore, avoid these mistakes which keto-ers often tend to make.

Firstly, you need to understand that going keto doesn't mean that you have to go for a food strike. No, whenever you feel hungry, you need to eat. Start with eating non-starchy vegetables. Vegetables contained essential vitamins, fiber, and electrolytes that will prepare your body for some side effects of keto diet in your initial days.

Secondly, when ketone level rises in the blood, they are excreted out of the body through sweat and urine. This way, your body loses electrolyte at an increase. Therefore, it is important to stay hydrated throughout the day. Drink lots of water, take electrolyte by adding sea salt to your bone, or just have bone broth.

Lastly, fats in keto diet don't mean consuming all type of fats. You need to make sure that the fats you eat are healthy, non-processed fats. Your approach for keto food should be a clean and healthy meal based on whole foods like organic eggs, fish, butter, avocado, and coconut oil. In the same way, you can't eat processed meats.

ABOUT THE AUTHOR

Patricia Bohn is a well-known nutrition and health expert with over twenty years' experience in the field.

Based in Los Angeles, California, Patricia works as a freelance writer and nutrition educator.

She is passionate about healthy eating and improving lives through good nutrition. Patricia accepts that healthy and mindful eating is a way of life, a life-long diet.

Her goal is to share her knowledge and experience with other people. Hopefully, her books will help you improve your life.

Made in the USA
Monee, IL
24 February 2023